F1 RACING CONFIDENTIAL

F1 RACING CONFIDENTIAL

INSIDE STORIES FROM THE WORLD OF FORMULA ONE

GILES RICHARDS

Michael O'Mara Books Limited

This paperback edition first published in 2025
First published in Great Britain in 2024 by
Michael O'Mara Books Limited
9 Lion Yard
Tremadoc Road
London SW4 7NQ

Copyright © Giles Richards 2024

All rights reserved. You may not copy, store, distribute, transmit, reproduce or otherwise make available this publication (or any part of it) in any form, or by any means (electronic, digital, optical, mechanical, photocopying, recording, machine readable, text/data mining or otherwise), without the prior written permission of the publisher. Any person who does any unauthorized act in relation to this publication may be liable to criminal prosecution and civil claims for damages.

A CIP catalogue record for this book is available from the British Library.

This product is made of material from well-managed, FSC®-certified forests and other controlled sources. The manufacturing processes conform to the environmental regulations of the country of origin.

ISBN: 978-1-78929-738-6 in paperback print format
ISBN: 978-1-78929-557-3 in ebook format

1 2 3 4 5 6 7 8 9 10

Cover design by Natasha Le Coultre
Designed and typeset by Design23
Printed and bound by CPI Group (UK) Ltd, Croydon, CR0 4YY

www.mombooks.com

Dedicated to my Mother and Father, whose unceasing encouragement, belief and love has informed and shaped my entire life and without whom none of this would have been possible.

In loving memory

Patricia Ann Joan Richards
17 April 1933 – 30 December 2017

Charles Donald Richards
26 October 1931 – 12 February 1995

CONTENTS

FOREWORD BY DAMON HILL 11
INTRODUCTION 13

CHAPTER 1
THE TEAM PRINCIPALS
CHRISTIAN HORNER & TOTO WOLFF 19

CHAPTER 2
THE RACE STRATEGIST
RUTH BUSCOMBE 49

CHAPTER 3
THE DRIVER
LANDO NORRIS 61

CHAPTER 4
THE TECHNICAL DIRECTOR
JAMES ALLISON 73

CHAPTER 5
THE CHIEF ENGINEER
PAUL MONAGHAN 85

CHAPTER 6
THE RACE ENGINEER
TOM STALLARD 99

CHAPTER 7
THE TYRE ENGINEER
PETER MABON 113

CHAPTER 8
THE PERFORMANCE COACH
RUPERT MANWARING 125

CHAPTER 9
THE AERODYNAMICIST
MARIANNE HINSON 137

CHAPTER 10
THE MACHINIST
NEIL AMBROSE 151

CHAPTER 11
THE HEAD OF COMMS
MATT BISHOP 163

CHAPTER 12
THE PIT MECHANIC
FRAZER BURCHELL 179

CHAPTER 13
THE CFO
RUSSELL BRAITHWAITE 193

CHAPTER 14
THE LOGISTICS COORDINATOR
SARAH LACY-SMITH 207

CHAPTER 15
THE TECHNICIAN
JACK PARTRIDGE 219

CHAPTER 16
THE ACADEMY HEAD
GUILLAUME ROCQUELIN 233

CHAPTER 17
THE CHIEF MECHANIC
KARI LAMMENRANTA 245

CHAPTER 18
THE MARKETING DIRECTOR
VICTORIA JOHNSON 259

CHAPTER 19
THE ESPORT DRIVER
LUCAS BLAKELEY 273

ACKNOWLEDGEMENTS 287
PICTURE CREDITS 291
INDEX 293

FOREWORD

In the rock 'n' roll business, there is a slightly bitter acknowledgement of a universal rule about singers: they are the last people to arrive and the first people to leave. In F1, drivers are the singers in the band. They turn up last, take all the applause, and then jet off into the sunset with all the cash. I know this is true because I was one!

Perhaps this aphorism is a little harsh, but the principle holds in general. Racing drivers are there to put the finishing touches to a mountain of work that is laboriously and lovingly served up to them in almost perfect form so that they can fulfil their lifetime ambitions of competing at the pinnacle of motorsport. They sound pretty insufferable when you put it like that, but please know that drivers are not the monsters I have depicted. They are acutely aware of the efforts put in by the armies of professionals on their teams, each of whom has their own personal ambitions and dreams to fulfil.

F1 is a not just a team sport, it is a system every bit as complex and fascinating as a termite colony. Actually, make that an entire ecosystem. For example, the guys and girls that do the logistics do not have the qualifications to design and build a racing car – they are another species entirely. But without their understanding of the sport and its complex and urgent needs, F1 simply could not function as it does. Every role in this multifaceted sport has a unique and valuable contribution to make to the whole. I have noticed in F1 that there are not a lot of people standing around doing nothing. Efficiency is the key.

When the cars cross the line on a Sunday they often have fireworks and a big celebration. The top three drivers climb the podium and spray champagne. But over the last few years it has been traditional for a member of the winning team to climb up there with them to be celebrated for their otherwise quiet contribution. They often look awkward, uncomfortable with the limelight. They just want to do their job well. And they have! But I always get a shiver of pride down my spine on these occasions because everyone works so hard for so long to get to that point. The celebrations are not just about the winner of the race or the winning team. They're about the whole show. They're about everyone, including the fans. We all do our bit, but the really hard work is done by the people in this book, who love their jobs and give that little bit extra because they care about doing something well. This book tells their stories.

And about time too!

Damon Hill, January 2024

INTRODUCTION

There are within this book, what I hope the reader will agree, a series of some fascinating, some unusual, some intriguing and many unique stories of the lives behind the people in Formula One and what they do in the most technologically advanced but also, at its heart, very human sport in the world.

These are the stories in F1 that are rarely, if ever, told and are largely from behind the scenes. They describe lives defined by great personal effort, of determination and of dedication. It must be hoped that the generosity, honesty and openness of the participants will prove inspiring to another generation of the sport to come.

That they all agreed to share their stories was in itself a great gesture and one of no little pluck. With the obvious exceptions of the most high-profile characters in this book, almost all of the participants do not usually speak to the media and the teams as a rule try to avoid adding pressure to their already high-intensity jobs by keeping them well away from microphones.

They have no media training, as the drivers do, and their day jobs do not include any expectation of, or experience in, being subjected to extended interviews, much of which were quite personal.

However, their overwhelmingly positive reaction to the process changed the very nature of this book swiftly after it had begun. Originally, the intention had been to give an account of what all these F1 personnel did, to take what are vital roles about which little is often known and bring them to a wider audience.

Almost immediately, however, it became clear there was so much more here. The most striking realization was that even as a lifelong F1 fan I found myself drawn to their stories as much as what they actually did. From a range of truly diverse backgrounds, their childhoods, tales of how they came to love F1, the many, some quite extraordinary, routes into the sport and what it felt like to finally find themselves working in it were fascinating.

These were accounts almost completely devoid of cliché because they had not been told dozens of times before; they felt vibrant, fresh and they had not been rehearsed to take all the rough edges off.

The purpose of the book was to make F1 as accessible as possible, to explain as clearly as possible to anyone coming to the sport for the first time and indeed long-time fans what was behind the garage door. F1 is without doubt a sport which, from the lexicon, through the rule book, to the labyrinthine nature of race strategy, takes an almost unhealthy pleasure in its technical complexity, in the arcane and the obscure.

Explaining the roles of key personnel and how their race weeks worked or their part in ensuring the team goes racing remained a key objective then, but it was clear that this was all the more approachable to a reader if there was an affinity with the subject. Their lives very much made them relatable and made said jobs all the more understandable from a human perspective.

The other major shift in emphasis this prompted was that it all sounded so much better in their own voices. Rather than reams of descriptive text laying out what, for example, a race engineer does, so interesting and expressive was every participant that their own words were far better than any amount of keyboard bashing on my behalf. It was clear that to let them do the talking as much as possible was the way forward and I have endeavoured to make sure that they are very much the voice of this book.

They seemed to enjoy this approach and a repeated refrain throughout all the interviews was a hope that their stories would encourage kids of all backgrounds to see F1 as something they could aspire to; itself indicative of how much they love the sport and how much they want it to be inclusive.

There was, without exception, not one interviewee that did not in the course of our conversations bring new insight, drawing back the curtain on many areas F1 has traditionally kept at arm's length. Nor indeed was there one of them that did not make me laugh as they described their lives and their roles, such was the good humour with which they took the relentless questioning.

There are stories within then that have never been told and I am proud to have played a small part in doing so, particularly as F1 has always been part of my life, albeit given that my journey to this point has been far more prosaic than the subjects herein.

There are moments surely for us all that remain indelibly etched in memory. For me, one was watching F1 in the mid to late 1970s as a six-year-old. Races coming in highlight form from impossibly exotic places; Brazil, yes, but also, well, Spain and Germany. At the time there were three TV channels and going to France was considered a major foreign trip. When James Hunt won the title at Fuji in Japan in 1976, he might well have won it on the moon as far as I was concerned. I knew Japan existed. The idea of ever going there was almost absurd.

After each race had concluded I would immediately try and recreate a new one using toy cars, a circuit defined by pieces of wooden toy train tracks and a die, each roll allocating a movement distance to the competitors based on their length. Roll a six and you moved six car lengths.

That the cars involved would vary from a little Mini Cooper to some extreme drag racing monster was irrelevant. On the carpet were toy cars of every size and shape. I recall Muttley and Dick Dastardly's car from *Wacky Races* was in there, which the FIA would doubtless have had issues with, but it didn't matter because in my mind it was F1 in all its glorious, exotic beauty.

The winner – and there never was a winner because bedtime always interrupted an absolutely classic battle and the track and competitors were back in the toy box by the next day – was irrelevant. What mattered was the racing and that was what I loved about F1.

Those moments have stayed with me ever since and they're one reason why this book exists. The fascination I felt then never really left me; some things never do. I remember with equal clarity my first gig. The Damned at Portsmouth Guildhall on 14 June 1985. It too is seared in my brain – the noise, the sweat from a heaving crowd in front of the stage. I left with ears ringing and a lifelong love of music that has remained a constant, alongside F1.

I went on to play in a band and study political science, but all the time there was F1 still demanding attention every Sunday and when, years later, I ended up covering the sport it felt a little like I had come home. The kid on the carpet playing with cars was actually watching it happen. Every time I attend a race I go trackside to watch, and when on the grid the experience still feels a little unreal. I know it is an enormous privilege and one not taken for granted, but it has perhaps been an even greater honour to be able to share the stories of the people who make it all happen.

CHAPTER 1

THE TEAM PRINCIPALS

The team principal is surely the most complex, multi-faceted role in F1. Not only are they the team leader but also must choose and manage the drivers and the convoluted and antagonistic politics of F1, to be then if necessary a father figure, a diplomat, negotiator and defender of their corner. They represent and direct a workforce of between 800 and 1,500 people and a budget commensurate with that vast resource. They must motivate, delegate, manage morale and be business-minded enough to please sponsors, all the while keeping an eye on pleasing the fans. They are the public-facing figurehead of the team and thus responsible for handling the media and, of course, are where the buck stops in terms of responsibility in a sport where the pressure to succeed is intense and failure is given short shrift indeed.

It is a precarious balancing act of maintaining myriad balls in the air while also concurrently observing an expansive, long-term, strategic picture and it is a task suited to very few, hence usually attracting distinctive personalities. Mercedes' Toto Wolff and Red Bull's Christian Horner have mastered it like no others in the modern era. Since 2010, between them they have won every Drivers' and Constructors' Championship and have become the most scrutinized team leaders in the sport. They are charismatic personalities, and each has a distinctive story to tell, but both offer a unique insight into what it takes to be a successful team principal.

CHRISTIAN HORNER
TEAM PRINCIPAL - ORACLE RED BULL RACING

'I feel fortunate, very fortunate. I am grateful every day for the job that I have, the people I work with. I never, ever take it for granted; if you do, complacency sets in. There is a fear of failure that drives you, you know what success feels like and it almost becomes addictive. You just want to have that feeling again.'

There can be no doubting quite how driven Christian Horner is in pursuit of that success, such that it is all-consuming and as he says, positively compelling. If he truly does have any fears – and it is hard to imagine from someone who radiates a sense of quiet confidence and self-belief – then perhaps it really is only that of failure. As he speaks of the addictive nature of winning, he smiles, his eyes sparkle, as if the very thought of it delivers a Pavlovian pleasure response. Little wonder given his remarkable achievements with Red Bull as a team principal who still revels in his task.

Having joined Red Bull as principal in the team's first season in F1 in 2005, at thirty-one years old Horner was the youngest ever team principal at the time. Almost two decades later he remains with the team and is now the longest-serving principal on the grid. From being the perceived upstart, the whippersnapper who had never worked in F1 before, to leading one of the biggest teams in modern F1, he has overseen one of the sport's great success stories.

Horner is easily recognized, his still youthful face familiar to fans, as is his assured, assertive manner. They know Horner in place on the pit wall overseeing the race, his leg pumping on the perch with echoes of the same intense, nervous energy Joe Strummer displayed, pounding the stage with the Clash. His achievements with Red Bull make for a formidable record. They have now won thirteen titles – seven Drivers' and six Constructors' Championships – with Horner at the helm in a role he has learned from the seat of his pants as he went along, ever since he hung up his driving overalls.

He does not hesitate for a moment when asked to explain what he believes is the single most important consideration in successfully running an F1 team. 'It's a people business,' he says, emphatically. 'It's about understanding people and working with people; getting the best out of them, empowering people and working as a team. It's about getting the right people around you and giving them the right direction. It is communicating, talking with them, recognizing their skills and trying to create the right environment for them.'

Under Horner's direction, Sebastian Vettel won four titles for the team between 2010 and 2013 and Max Verstappen has now won a further three since 2021. Horner does not downplay the importance of the drivers. They are required to deliver behind the wheel and he knows well how decisive an exceptional talent can be in a car, but he returns to his point in order to stress how they are only the tip of an immense effort being made across the board.

'The biggest thing for me is that you have the right spirit and the right desire within the team, then anything is possible,' he adds. 'Nobody envisaged when we started this journey of winning more than one hundred Grands Prix and thirteen World Championships, it was beyond our wildest dreams. It all comes down to the people and the desire and that philosophy that has served us so well.'

Red Bull have always made a point of trying to differentiate itself from more traditional teams. They have enjoyed their reputation as outcasts, 'the energy drink team' as they are sometimes referred to dismissively. Horner takes no slight in this, indeed he has embraced it and made it part of the philosophy to which he refers.

'We are different at Red Bull. You won't see anyone in a suit and tie here; it's more jeans and T-shirt,' he says of the culture he has engendered at the team. 'We play our music loud, we don't conform, and we are not answerable to an engine manufacturer. We call it as we see it and we are not afraid to have an opinion.'

This he maintains is also a two-way street that is vital such that anyone in the team feels they can contribute. 'We have a can-do attitude, that anything is possible,' he says. 'So everybody has a voice. If they have something to say they should feel they are empowered to do so. It is a very inclusive atmosphere and comes from the top down. Walk into any department and they enjoy what they do and that has demonstrated how a group of people in a bunch of industrial units in Milton Keynes can take on Mercedes-Benz, or Ferrari, or McLaren, and win.'

Away from that huge campus in Milton Keynes, the most public-facing aspect of the team principal role is that of managing their drivers. This is where the headlines are generated and is the focal point for most fans who like nothing more than a spot of needle and conflict between teammates and should that descend into an all-out bitter feud, well, bring on the drama, for all that is the bane of a team principal's life.

The competition between teammates is always intense. The first measure for any driver is how they perform against the man at the wheel of the exact same machinery across the garage. There is nowhere to hide from the data that displays with uncompromising bluntness who is on top, relentlessly ratcheting up what are already fiercely competitive instincts.

For the team, where maximum points are the goal and teammates taking each other out is an ignominy deemed unacceptable, handling this delicate relationship can prove to be one of the trickiest tasks, especially where titles are on the line and roaring egos must be managed. Horner has dealt with it repeatedly, often at crunch points, and identifies that an ability to adapt according to the needs of each individual is vital.

'The word teammate is a bit of a fallacy because they are anything but mates, because one will dictate the other's worth,' he says, with a knowing smile. 'They are very competitive. Drivers are effectively contractors and they have their own objectives and desires, but the most important thing for the team is not only the Drivers' Championship but where the money is paid which is from where you finish in the Constructors' Championship.

'So before you have started you already have that conflict of interest. They are very driven, and they are selfish and uncompromising. So different drivers require a different approach. Sebastian [Vettel] was very much an arm around the shoulder kind of guy. Max [Verstappen] in comparison is very straightforward. Then you might have a Mark Webber or a Sergio Pérez; they are all different.'

Indeed, when Vettel and Webber were vying with one another during those four title-winning years, their rivalry grew so fractious and intense that Horner had to find inventive ways to deal with them. After the pair collided at the Turkish Grand Prix in 2010, he felt he had to intervene.

'Sometimes you have to disarm them,' he explains. 'We live in a bubble that can become so self-obsessed and absorbed, so I wanted to take them out of that to see somebody with real-life issues. I wanted them to have a better perspective on life in general so I took them to Great Ormond Street Children's Hospital to meet a bunch of kids who were having a tough time and parents who were having an equally tough time.

'It was a bit of a reality check, to say: "Look, guys, you have it pretty good, you are well paid, doing a job you love. You are not saving lives, if you think you have it hard, these kids have it hard." It was an eye-opener for them.'

The experience was beneficial for both men and their relationship, but that it is a Sisyphean task for the principal to maintain a harmonious garage was also demonstrated when the relationship between the two effectively disintegrated over the Multi-21 team orders incident in Malaysia in 2013.

On that occasion, Vettel defied team orders to stay behind Webber, overtaking his teammate. Yet even this was viewed by Horner as another opportunity to learn from, to hone the people management techniques that he values so highly – a process of deriving skills from experience that he began developing long before rising to team principal, having started his career behind the wheel of a go-kart.

The fifty-year-old grew up just outside Leamington Spa and recollects distinctly the moment he found motor racing. 'I remember first watching on TV in 1984,' he recalls. 'It was when Nigel Mansell spun off after hitting a white line in the Monaco Grand Prix in the pouring rain. I was drawn into it, and Nigel was the growing hero at that time.'

Always fascinated by speed, Horner made his own soapbox go-karts to run down the hill at the back of the village and when he was twelve relentlessly pestered his mother for a motorized version, having observed that: 'She was a bit softer than my father.'

With Mum persuaded, they bought a beaten-up 1970s Zip Kart, a model which was designed, unbeknown to the family, for racing. Too low to drive in the garden then, he moved from a car park to the Shenington kart track where Mansell had begun his career – another key moment. 'Suddenly I discovered the world of kart racing. The kart we had was hopelessly out of date but it was a fantastic starting point,' he says.

A year later his parents bought him a newer kart and he admits he became addicted to racing, if in a manner that might not have pleased them. 'I had the engine in my bedroom for a month, and it stank the house out,' he recalls with a laugh. 'I just wanted it in my bedroom. Like any boy's dream, I would just visualize myself as an F1 driver. I kept scrapbooks, all of Nigel's cuttings, cut out all the newspaper stuff, and my parents still have them.'

Showing real promise, from karts he graduated to single seaters in Formula Renault, enjoying a win and some poles, then moved into British F3 where he also enjoyed success, winning races, before then in 1997 stepping up to Formula 3000. Without the budget to buy a seat, Horner opted instead to buy a car and run his own team, and Arden International was formed. Horner did everything: drove, managed the money, the organization, the food, the travel.

It was crucial experience, especially when he chose to hang up the helmet at the end of 1998. At just twenty-five years old it was an early example of his clear-sighted pragmatism. 'I was honest with myself,' he says. 'I recognized that the higher you got in the categories, the faster the cars become, and there was a realization you could actually hurt yourself. I had a self-preservation mechanism and I recognized that I was alright, but I didn't have the ability of a Juan Pablo Montoya, or a Tom Kristensen, or a Nick Heidfeld, the kind of guys I was racing at that time.'

Still enjoying the challenge of running the team, however, Horner decided instead to continue to make a go of Arden as team principal and owner. He took them from strength to strength. They won the Formula 3000 drivers' title in 2002, 2003 and 2004, albeit that first one was a salutary lesson in what was required from driver management after Tomáš Enge won only to have points deducted for failing a drugs test for marijuana, costing him the title.

'I learned some hugely important lessons, especially about people,' says Horner. 'It was about getting the best engineers, the best technicians and getting them to work as a team. Even though it was only around twenty people, it was still a matter of getting the right ones. I had nothing to lose at that point and I took some horrendous financial risks to get the right drivers in the car. I ended up living on credit cards, robbing Peter to pay Paul.'

Yet his determination paid off and when he considered making the step up to F1, encouraged to do so by Bernie Ecclestone, other parties had been taking notice. After a potential purchase of Eddie Jordan's eponymous team came to nothing – 'We did due diligence on Eddie's team but very quickly decided against it,' he recalls – he was approached by Red Bull's director of motorsport Helmut Marko who introduced him to Dietrich Mateschitz, the owner of the energy drink company who had bought out Jaguar at the end of 2004. Mateschitz offered Horner the principal role which he accepted, recognizing it was a potentially life-changing opportunity.

The team he inherited, however, was in far from great shape and had been underperforming for years. Indeed, Mateschitz offered Horner a bonus if they could just score more than the ten points Jaguar had amassed in 2004, a challenge he would meet with Red Bull scoring thirty-four in that first year.

The workforce then amounted to around 450 people who had seen a revolving door of management and turning it around was a daunting task. 'The scale was significantly bigger than I was used to in F3000 and on the day I was introduced to the business, the previous management were escorted from the building,' Horner remembers of what was something of a baptism of fire. 'So I walked in, and the assistant was in tears, former team principal Tony Purnell's half-drunk coffee was on his desk, there were unopened Christmas cards and a fairly disgruntled workforce. I thought: "OK, where do I start?"'

The somewhat humble beginnings make the achievements at Red Bull all the more remarkable. Horner used his experience at Arden and set about the task of putting the right people in place. One in particular was a master stroke and remains perhaps Red Bull's greatest asset. As a long-time fan of the hugely successful designer Adrian Newey, Horner immediately set about bringing him to Red Bull from McLaren. It was an absolutely pivotal moment so early in his time in charge and one pursued with single-minded determination that would benefit the team on a broad front.

'I felt if I could get Adrian then that would open the doors to other talent,' explains Horner. 'I was able to convince him it was the right move but I don't think he had any idea of what he was getting himself into. Then it was a question of, we need to build a team, build a structure. Adrian gave us that technical direction and it was up to us to make sure he had what he needed.'

With Newey on board in 2006 and the team building under way, Horner embraced the leadership style he had adopted and that he remains faithful to today.

'Being team principal is about understanding people, empowering people, getting the best out of them,' he says. 'There is no point in employing an Adrian Newey and then telling him how to do his job. So it's about recognizing people's skills, and trying to create the right environment to get the most out of them so that they feel valued.'

How this is achieved as the business has grown and grown – Red Bull now employ 1,500 people within Red Bull Racing, Red Bull Powertrains and Red Bull Advanced Technologies, across all three of which Horner sits as CEO – requires distinct and dynamic leadership defined by a high level of trust and autonomy.

'You have a strong management team in each of those pillars,' he says. 'A clear and effective structure. They all have a decent degree of autonomy, and you have to back them and put trust in them. If you try to control everything you will fail. I can set the tempo, the direction and objectives, but it is down to the individual to deliver. They have responsibility and accountability.'

There are of course areas within which the team principal cannot exercise quite as much influence and where character and adaptability play a vital role. F1 is political perhaps like no other team sport. Each team has its own agenda, pitting them against each other, but also while subject to relations with the governing body, the FIA, and the sport's commercial rights holder, Formula One Management. It is a triumvirate of labyrinthine complexity that must be navigated week in and week out.

'It is a necessary evil within the job,' Horner says. 'F1 is a highly contentious, highly political environment, whether it be with the commercial rights holder or the governing body or other teams. So it is part of the game and my job is to protect the team, to do the best I can for the team, to go into bat to ensure that they are protected and represented.'

Much of this happens behind closed doors, especially with the FIA and Formula One Management, but it is the public side, the relations with other team principals, that is the most rousing interaction as they fight their corner with the same intensity their drivers display on track.

Which is not to say the sparring, the toing and froing, does not bring a frisson of pleasure to the protagonists. 'It doesn't faze me – it's a bit of sport isn't it,' says Horner. 'If you have a competitor who is getting a bit wound up and throwing a few bombs, if you can disarm them in a public forum, well. When you see a competitor smashing up headphones or pointing at cameras, visibly losing it in front of a camera, you think: "OK, we are under your skin."'

The undertone – that he is referring to Toto Wolff and moments in their increasingly fractious relationship in the 2021 season – is clear. That year during an extremely competitive fight between Verstappen and Lewis Hamilton for the title, their scrap was made only more gripping as Horner and Wolff vied publicly with one another, each attempting to score points, to manoeuvre on to the psychological high ground. Which, for all that it made for ribald entertainment, also had a serious subtext.

'If they are losing it publicly, at that point if they are behaving like that within their team environment then people around them are going to be feeling that and it permeates from the top,' Horner observes. 'So that will make people tense and tighten up. [Former Manchester United manager] Alex Ferguson was the master of it within his field. I'm not saying I am an Alex Ferguson but the competition is fierce and when it gets to a competition like we had in 2021, that was as much off track as it was on track.'

This arena, known as the 'Piranha Club', echoes to the sound of these egos clashing. Team principals are very rarely shrinking violets, reticent about getting stuck into a fight. Yet Horner also maintains that for all the puffing of chests, of the accusations and counter-accusations, the trick is not to let it distract from the real task.

'I don't think it is arrogance but you have to have inner confidence and belief in yourself,' he says. 'Yet the biggest thing I have learned over almost twenty years of this job is to worry about the things you can control and influence rather than the things you can't.'

Exerting that control also requires a level of ruthlessness, an ability to acknowledge when structures and personnel must change, however difficult it may be, perhaps most notably observed with a pitiless eye in the drivers' market. All teams are measured by results and if a driver is not returning what was expected, they can expect to be removed – there is no room for sentimentality in such a competitive field.

In 2016, having already taken a chance in bringing Verstappen into Red Bull's sister team Toro Rosso as the youngest F1 driver at seventeen years and 166 days old, Horner felt he had to act decisively to deal with an underperforming Daniil Kvyat within his team. He switched Kvyat with Verstappen in only the Dutch teenager's second season, a move that was considered very risky at the time but one Horner felt he could not shy away from. He was duly vindicated in spectacular style when Verstappen won the Spanish Grand Prix on his first outing for Red Bull.

'Sometimes difficult decisions have to be made and sometimes they are unpopular,' Horner says. 'But you have to do what's right for the team. It's not about popularity, it's about where you are on a Sunday afternoon.

'On one hand you're taking a driver's dreams away from them, but on the other hand you are doing what is right for the team, so of course it was an unpopular decision at the time but it was absolutely the right thing to do because not only did it secure longevity with Max but he won his first Grand Prix. You are constantly managing risks and looking at risk versus reward; the risk in doing that was pretty minor but the upside was pretty significant if he delivered on the promise we believed that he had.'

Horner's commitment to the team is palpably absolute but he also observes how important it is to be able to step away from it. He views downtime away from the sport with his family as crucial. The personal sense of responsibility he feels for the team is set aside to ensure quality time with his loved ones, a process he insists allows clearer thought and decision-making when back on the job.

This is doubly necessary he maintains because of the relentless demands the role entails. 'As an individual you try and compartmentalize things, but the pressure is inevitable,' he says. 'In the 2021 season, the pressure during that year was to a level that I had not seen before. It was more to do with what was going on off the track – the lobbying, the politics – as opposed to what was going on on the track.

'It was only when the chequered flag fell in Abu Dhabi that suddenly you feel this enormous sense of relief. You have been carrying it all year and it is building and it is building and you carry a lot of it to protect the people that are around you to enable them to do their job so they don't feel it. It's only at a moment like that that you feel this huge burden just lift; I felt it physically.'

Yet for all that burden, the responsibility that can weigh heavy, for Horner this is the very essence of the role and what has long kept him motivated. At the very top of an F1 team, success and failure go hand in hand with a sincere devotion to the sport that can be felt right across the grid.

'Of course you see the role as personal, because if you didn't take it personally it would show you didn't care,' he says with heartfelt conviction. 'If you are just doing it because it is a job you are in the wrong sport. It's not a nine-to-five job, or business, it has to be a passion. If you are passionate about something you just do it that much better; you put your heart and soul into it.'

TOTO WOLFF
TEAM PRINCIPAL & CEO - MERCEDES-AMG PETRONAS F1 TEAM

'The sense of team, that mindset and the collaboration is so important. Even if you are fighting with inferior weapons, infrastructure and technology, if you stick together, then you can move heaven and earth. You could say that technology and engineering make your car fast and that wins you races, but there is much more. There is the human angle, the emotions and the will of giving it all. I believe this is what we all created together at Mercedes.'

A belief in the positivity of working collectively, creating a harmonious whole in an exactingly demanding environment towards a common goal is fundamental for Toto Wolff and a refrain to which he often returns when he considers his position as an F1 team principal and CEO.

Indeed, it becomes clear it is far more than a mere management technique or a construct around which to base decision-making. For Wolff it is a character trait that has informed his career and has helped deliver extraordinary success to his Mercedes team since he joined them in 2013.

Even then, back before he led them to eight consecutive Constructors' titles and seven Drivers' Championships, Wolff was absolutely committed to the team to the exclusion of almost all else.

'One of the advantages and perhaps disadvantages of my character is that I take everything personally,' he says. 'When I joined, the team became my tribe; it was all-encompassing. Every day, the minute I woke up to the minute I fell asleep it was all I did. Caring about the people, about what we needed to *be* in order to be successful. It is what I do and when I do it I forget about everything around me.'

It is telling that Wolff says what we needed to 'be' rather than needed to 'do', his own emphasis indicating the centrality of the people and the culture to the task. He threw himself into it with an altogether unsurprising dedication and since then, as one of the three biggest teams in F1, has seen his responsibilities evolve to become greater and greater still alongside the success. He has had to manage fractious driver pairings, testing and, on occasion, devastating disappointment on the track, an exponential growth in the size of his team as well as, of course, the endless politicking in F1 in fighting his corner for his team and every employee for whom he feels a personal responsibility.

Wolff is charming and witty, often enjoying a deadpan sense of humour that is endearing. He is also honest, unafraid to hold his hands up to errors and willing to engage in debate rather than fall back on banality. His brow will sometimes furrow as he seeks the best words to express himself in English, a second language to his native Austrian German and when he finds it, it is usually worth the wait in correctly articulating his feelings. Close friends with Niki Lauda, the great triple world champion was more outspoken, but Wolff has learned from how engaging Lauda was as well as his incisive analysis.

At fifty-two years old, he shoulders a team that has been both at the very top of F1 and also fighting to return to those heights. A team that over the past decade has roughly doubled in size. In 2013 it employed around 520 people at the Mercedes High Performance Powertrains engine facility in Brixworth and 660 at the Mercedes F1 team. Today the total number across the organization is 2,500, while over the same period sponsorship revenue has grown from £50 million a year in 2013 to over £300 million today. The sheer size and import of the two organizations suggests that managing it would be an exacting and exhausting task. Yet Wolff insists the challenge, the intensity of competition, is carried lightly.

'I have never felt pressure, never in my life,' he says. 'I take calculated risks that mean I can cope with the worst outcome. If the worst outcome would really influence the quality of my life I would not take the decision.

'If you have the tough moments in your life that everyone has, F1 is a walk in the park in comparison. I feel zero pressure. All I feel is that I want to meet my own expectations and whether I achieve those objectives or not. That comes with emotions, including frustration and annoyance but only with myself. But no pressure.'

Wolff is indeed unafraid to embrace and show his emotions. He is invested in the sport and in his team, but given that he is also a keen student of assessing himself critically, he is also aware that they have to be channelled and controlled.

'I have always been emotional,' he adds. 'But I try to contain that in the best possible way.'

That he gives his passion relatively free rein is a trait that has proved enormously efficacious in the realm of driver management and in particular with one of F1's greatest talents. When Wolff joined Mercedes in 2013, Lewis Hamilton also made his switch to the team from McLaren.

He won a race for them in that first season and with the advent of the turbo-hybrid era the following year and Mercedes delivering a car and engine that were the class of the field, he would win a title 2014 and deliver five more by 2020. The team would take eight Constructors' Championships between 2014 and 2021 and Hamilton and Wolff were on the journey alongside one another, learning together and during which they have developed a very special relationship that is unusual in F1.

Hamilton and Wolff share a professional bond but also something far more profound in a genuine friendship that gives each a unique insight into the other and an understanding that is hugely beneficial to the team as a whole.

'We have been together for eleven years, we are friends and we are allies and that encompasses the full range of emotions in a relationship,' says Wolff. 'We know each other so well, and we have gone through hard times in our relationship, tough times in our lives that we have shared with each other and great moments together. That means you can put yourself in each other's shoes. I can reflect on why Lewis is thinking a certain way and that has been a very strong bond between us. I know what Lewis needs and what Lewis wants.

'Equally good friends can also have hard arguments with each other. We are able to disagree whilst not falling out with each other. He understands that I need to act in the interest of the team and I understand that a driver needs to act for the best of his interests. He is strong in the car but also a strong team member as well.'

Their friendship demonstrates what can be forged with longevity, but there are two drivers in every team and handling them both and their relationship with one another is a key part of the team principal's role. Wolff entered driver management in the early part of his career as co-owner of a sports management company that counted Pastor Maldonado, Bruno Senna, Rubens Barrichello and Nico Hulkenberg among its clients. Being involved with the management of these drivers, advancing their careers was his aim. At Mercedes, however, the task has been altogether different, focused on maintaining the maximum from both Hamilton and his then teammate Nico Rosberg. Not an easy endeavour especially as the pair's relationship in vying with one another for the World Championship became increasingly irascible.

Wolff brought his overarching philosophy of team over all immediately to bear. 'At Mercedes, because Lewis and Nico were big stars and I was relatively new to F1, it was an interesting journey for me,' he says. 'But straight from the beginning I said to them and to everyone that I am not having two superstars; I have a thousand superstars. I register no difference between any single employee and the drivers.'

Hamilton and Rosberg clashed on track at Belgium and Monaco in 2014, there was ill temper and a spot of handbags after Hamilton took the title in Texas in 2015, and famously they took each other out of the race in Barcelona in 2016, the year Rosberg would go on to win his only title. The pair had been friends as youngsters in karting but the relationship came apart, perhaps unsurprisingly. These are strong characters that are hard to contain, and it is very much part of what makes them special, as Wolff observes.

'Well there is ego but I really like ego because ego is a strong driver,' he says. 'But it needs to be channelled, it needs to be conditioned. Ego needs to be contained, not completely but to a certain degree. I believe the best performers have ego, they have edges but that makes them very strong.'

Nor does he confine this assessment only to drivers. 'There are so many egos in F1, so many strong characters within the team. It's not only Lewis and George Russell,' he adds. 'There are so many good engineers, so many good managers in the team, where I need to condition the strong ego and I don't mean that as a negative. So much personality management is to try to keep the mindset of the lion within people without it being detrimental for the wider environment.'

Wolff is emphatic that this task of allowing his team the freedom to work and express themselves, to consider every option and think independently, to let the lion roar as he intimates, is one he sees as vital in drawing the best from everyone. To that end he also sees a level of plain speaking and honesty as a crucial element and it is something he had to address from the moment he started at Mercedes, delivering some uncomfortable truths to the Mercedes-Benz board.

The team had evolved from Ken Tyrrell's outfit that raced with enormous success in the 1960s and 1970s with Sir Jackie Stewart taking three drivers' titles. It was sold to British American Racing in 1998 who relocated their base to Brackley where the team is still based today. Honda took over in 2006 until they too exited suddenly in 2009 and it was acquired as Brawn GP by the then team principal Ross Brawn. Jenson Button took the drivers' title that year and the team the constructors', at the end of which they were bought out by Mercedes as the marque returned to F1 with a works team for the first time since 1955.

When in 2013 Wolff arrived from his previous role as executive director at Williams, he identified two areas that needed to be urgently addressed. The first was straightforward and something he could influence directly. 'One major issue was to look at mindset building and the team cohesion; that was one fundamental block,' he says.

The second, however, was more complex. The Austrian had been asked to assess the team in the summer of 2012, specifically in reference as to why they had not been more successful. What Wolff discovered did not please the board. Their expectations were, having bought a championship-winning team, that they would win championships.

'I told them: "I am at Williams running exactly the same budgets and my expectation is top six and you have the same budget and your expectation is world champions – that's what is wrong,"' he said. 'They were very angry but I said: "Don't shoot the messenger ..."

'So when I came in I told Mercedes I need to have the same budget as our main competitors, Ferrari and Red Bull. I won't guarantee that this will make us win the championship, but I can guarantee that if you don't give it to us you will not win it. That was the decisive moment and the board said: "Tell us what you need."'

The expense may not have been in the original Mercedes plan, but the extraordinary success that followed doubtless more than made up for it. Wolff had displayed the same critical honesty that he had applied to his own career that ultimately set him down the path to F1 for all that he had no idea that it would be his destination.

He was born in Vienna in 1972 but had no interest in motor racing growing up other than being aware of course of fellow Austrian Lauda. Indeed it was not until he was eighteen that he actually experienced motor racing, but when he did it had an overwhelming impact.

On a weekend away with friends, he stopped at the Nürburgring to watch an F3 race. Wolff's visceral reaction to it startled him. 'I remember walking on to the grid and standing next to those F3 cars and I was thunderstruck, realizing this is what I wanted to do,' he says.

He describes it as 'the moment I found my identity' and was captivated by it. 'It was a defining moment in my life, if not one of the most important moments of my life,' he recalls. 'I don't remember watching the race but it was the drivers, in those cars on the grid, ready to go in their machines. What excited me was driving these cars and I wanted to do it immediately, but I didn't even know where to start.'

Typically Wolff just threw himself into it to find out. He gained sponsors, bought a Seat Ibiza, attended the Walter Lechner racing school and took to the track. He then moved to a Formula Ford 1600 but was unlucky at the very opening race in Brno. After a spin he was T-boned by another car, the bones in his fingers were smashed and he was taken to a nearby hospital in what was then Czechoslovakia that had only just thrown off the yoke of Soviet control. The incident has unsurprisingly stayed, quite vividly, with him.

'I was in this ex-communist hospital,' he recalls. 'They were doing my X-ray and there was no protection. The X-ray machine looked like an antique and they said to me: 'Operazion'. So I call my mother who is an anaesthesiologist and I tell her I broke my hand, and she says: "You idiot. I told you it was a waste of money."

'I told her they want to operate on me and she just says: "Get out of there!" So I am there in my hospital dressing gown and I put on my trousers and ran outside. I jumped in my car and drove to Vienna, a two-hour drive with broken fingers, one-handed, flat out.

He duly had a successful 'operazion' in Vienna to conclude what he describes laughingly as his 'first Formula Ford racing adventure'.

More would follow and he dearly loved racing but ultimately Wolff's pragmatic side won out over his driving ambitions. He accepted he had started late in his life and was struggling to quite match his contemporaries so decided to call it a day and strike out anew in 1994.

'With my critical self-assessment I decided just to stop,' he explains. 'I felt rather than being on the back foot I am going to stop studying and stop racing. I am going to launch myself into business so I am the first one that starts work. That's what I did and I never looked back.'

It was a bold but ultimately inspired decision in being far more successful in business than he was behind the wheel. He worked up to setting up a venture capital fund and racing disappeared off the radar until 1999 when he was twenty-six. A one-off invitation from a friend to take part in an endurance race, once more in Brno, piqued his interest and reminded Wolff of his love of racing.

So he took it up again sporadically in GTs and rallying and began investing in teams at that level, including the HWA DTM (German Touring Car) team, where he became an executive director. It led to a similar investment in the Williams F1 team and the place of executive director there, where he was effectively running the team alongside team principal and founder Frank Williams.

Mercedes were impressed. They came knocking and in 2013 Wolff was appointed executive director and became a shareholder in the team. It was, he says, a 'pinch yourself moment' and somewhat daunting.

'Before coming, Brackley – because I called them 'Team Brackley' – was a team of survivors,' he says. 'Because they survived racing, they survived Honda, they survived Brawn and they survived the transition to Mercedes in those years. So they were survivors, but there was not a sense of a team feeling that I thought a team should have. But they did have this very strong group that was there for a long time with a lot of expertise.

'What I tried to implement was coherence and team values. The right mindset, empowerment, a no-blame culture. I was totally immersed in every decision, be it technical or commercial.'

His initial plan was for a three-year role then to withdraw with his investment. It was rolled over for a further three years until in 2020 when he decided that it really was his calling and he went all in as a shareholder, who now owns an equal third of the team alongside Mercedes-Benz AMG and the chair of the Ineos chemical company headed by Sir Jim Ratcliffe. It was Wolff's total commitment to F1 and to Mercedes.

'I have always had long relationships and I knew if I took the decision, then this was a decision for life,' he says. 'It would no longer simply be an investment because I realized that F1 is my niche. I love what I do.'

The task clearly invigorates Wolff through good times, of which there have been many, but also through bad. That is part of competition and indeed what drives him, but the scale of this level of racing is like no other – it is team and it is business and between them it is an enormous undertaking. While he is attentive to every detail of the operation he is keenly aware he cannot be hands on with everything. As with all team principals he understands that delegation is fundamental. Given that is the case it is telling that he puts character at the very heart of assessing the suitability for responsibility of those around him.

'I employ people who share our values so I trust them,' he says. 'For me, personality is the most important and belief in the values that we share. That is integrity, loyalty, we don't deal in lies, we blame the problem and not the person, we empower whilst we choose carefully the people that we empower.'

There are some clear similarities here with Christian Horner's approach. The pair may be different personalities but it is instructive how in some areas their views intersect with one another, suggesting that though from differing backgrounds, their interpretation of management, particularly in relation to people, is similar and success has followed with it for both of them.

Wolff smiles as he considers the relationship with his rival and how their sparring has become as much a part of the show as the battling on track.

'It is happening under the magnifying glass of the media and a little bit is exaggerated, but obviously there is emotion involved also because we are both passionate about what we do,' he says. 'The two of us have been fighting for race victories and championships for ten years whilst representing our teams. We are different personalities, we have different values but even your worst enemy has a best friend and I acknowledge that and he is not my worst enemy. Because of what he has achieved I respect the achievement.'

Their competitive relationship reached its most intense moment at the Abu Dhabi Grand Prix in 2021 when controversial errors by then race director Michael Masi were instrumental in deciding the race, which was won by Max Verstappen, and in so doing denied Hamilton his eighth title. Wolff and Mercedes were incensed at the time and it appears it must have been the most difficult moment to have dealt with in his career, but while it clearly still rankles he insists it must be considered in context.

'It's important for me to be able to put it into perspective and in that light it certainly wasn't the hardest moment that I had in my life; there were a hundred that were harder than this,' he says. 'I also understand that there are far worse tragedies happening in the world – look at what is happening in Ukraine.'

Which is a sober, mature evaluation that is unsurprising from Wolff, but the sense of injustice he feels from that day does nonetheless remain.

'What happened was extreme unfairness in a sport that should be fair. I felt disbelief in the decision-making, when you realize that one person can take the position away through their mistakes, with all the work that has been put in by many, many people and Lewis in building this. They change the outcome of F1 history. All the competence, the hard work, the commitment of many people can still go in the bin within a few seconds because someone takes a bad decision.'

As he has made clear, Wolff is self-admittedly an emotional character and it seems doubtful he will ever throw off his grievance at the events, but it is also clear that they form only a tiny part of the rich tapestry that has made up his career. That overall there is enormous satisfaction and indeed anticipation of more to come.

'Life is full of surprises. I would never have imagined I would be here or the success of this team,' he says. 'I am fifty-two now. It sounds like an old age but hopefully there are another thirty years of Mercedes F1 for me. It's important that when you hand over the baton at eighty, you can say: "That was pretty good. I am happy with myself – I met my own expectations of my life."'

CHAPTER 2

THE RACE STRATEGIST

RUTH BUSCOMBE
HEAD OF RACE STRATEGY - ALFA ROMEO F1 TEAM STAKE

'Three days into my university career I was hit by a speeding car. It was the best and worst thing that ever happened to me. The physical and mental recuperation from it was incredibly hard, from trying to walk again to trying to study in between hospital and taking painkillers. But with the friends I made along the way I learned that you are not an island, sometimes maybe a peninsula, but you are never an island. It changed my path and ultimately turned me into the person I am today.'

Ruth Buscombe does not shy away from addressing the harrowing events that shaped her life before F1; indeed, typically for this focused, determined and enormously positive young woman, she insists they only made her stronger. After arriving at Cambridge to take the degree she hoped would propel her into the sport she loved, she was hospitalized following being hit by a car while on her bicycle. It could not have been more serious and she had to undergo life-saving surgery, an experience that has given her perspective on everything that has followed in a remarkable career.

As a rule, however, Buscombe does not dwell too much on the past. She follows the account of what happened with an example of the self-deprecating humour and *joie de vivre* that peppers her conversation and makes her hugely endearing company. 'I still beep every time I go through airport security,' she says, with a laugh. 'Because my ankle is made of metal.'

Buscombe had gone to Cambridge to study engineering, specifically because she had learned that this is what technical directors such as Mercedes' James Allison had done. For this singular woman, who had left absolutely nothing to chance since she had chosen F1 as her career when she was still a schoolgirl, a life-threatening accident was not going to derail her ambitions.

Having made it to F1, working for Ferrari and then Haas, she went on to become Head of Strategy at Alfa Romeo F1 Team Stake. On the pit wall she calls the shots during a race, and when the lights go out she has perhaps the most intensely pressurized role in the team, bar the drivers. A position where success might go unnoticed but failure, a bad call on strategy, is painfully obvious.

Buscombe is an object lesson in how far talent and a single-minded sense of purpose can take you and has proved an inspiration to those following in her footsteps. Her story is as fascinating as it is entertaining. Yet F1 was not the very first goal the thirty-four-year-old had in mind.

'I wanted to be a princess – something with a crown – or an astronaut,' she says with a smile. 'But I learned at that time you could only be an astronaut if you were an American or joined the RAF. I was a very practical ten-year-old and I did a lot of research and I was very annoying. I always liked problem-solving and my application to Cambridge was about F1 and Apollo 13, how I saw engineering as being about working out the problem and fitting a square into a circle.'

Buscombe grew up in London's East Ham with her parents who were both doctors and although as a West Ham United fan she preferred football, she was exposed to F1 by her dad who adored McLaren. 'He had control of the remote so that's how we always ended up with F1 on the TV,' she says. 'Over time I got used to watching it and got into it. You know, if you can't beat them, join them.

'Then when I worked out there were engineers and people doing maths, that was a penny-drop moment. I loved sport and I loved maths, so that was it for me – I was doomed from that point. It was the only thing I wanted to do and I was ten when I made that decision.'

Buscombe still speaks with a faint tinge of an East End accent and there is a welcome, frank honesty as she recalls how determined she was, having committed to making it to F1.

'I was a ridiculously driven child,' she says. 'I was moved up a year at primary school and I would get my parents to teach me extra maths so I would be ahead. I suppose I was a weird kid. I was very practical in that I felt having a dream without a plan was not a goal. I wanted to be pragmatic to work out what I needed to do to get into Cambridge.

'I was really good at maths – I was a mathlete, doing maths competitions. I excelled at maths, physics and science. I would get really mad at myself if I got 99 per cent in an exam. I have got less weird but at the time that's where I was at.'

There was, then, clearly no little focus from the girl who even then was well read. Buscombe's conversation is frequently illustrated with quotations from authors she admires or people who have inspired her. She cites tennis legend and gender equality advocate Billie Jean King's observation that 'pressure is a privilege' as an example of the incentive to study hard so you could make your point with a successful outcome. 'I loved exams, which I know is deeply uncool,' she says. 'But it's because the exam is the proof, the confirmation of all the work you have done before.'

Unsurprisingly, Buscombe threw herself into her task, taking six A levels and a host of extracurricular activities to improve her chances of making it to Cambridge. Enthused by her chosen path she was it seems a force of nature, driven by a desire to ensure she would not end up chained to a desk.

'I have never worried about determination,' she says. 'I was born with an abundance of determination, sometimes limited by time or sanity, but determination has never been an issue for me. I just don't think I could ever have done an office job. I think my soul would have withered away because I need the excitement.'

It paid off and with her place secured, Buscombe went to

Cambridge to pursue her dream, studying aerodynamic engineering.

However, she had barely opened a book before her entire future hung in the balance after the accident. Coming back from it was an astonishing feat, which she acknowledges today. 'People ask what I am most proud of. Was it graduating with a first-class degree? But I am more proud of getting through those first two years,' she says. 'When I was in and out of hospital, the experience, grit and determination that gave me, and the friendships and camaraderie that I had through that time meant so much.

'That's why my friends, who took pity on the hopalong at the back of the lecture theatre, mean so much to me. They took pity on the strange lady but to this day I don't remember meeting them the first time because I was on so many painkillers.'

It was a long, slow recovery, leaning on her friends, concerned about the volume of painkillers she was taking and trying all the while to continue to study around these issues. Yet it was a process which, with typical single-mindedness, Buscombe wanted to use to her advantage.

'It was something I had to reframe, something bad that I had to turn into an opportunity,' she explains. 'This is my chance to show how much I want something. We all want these traits – courage, bravery, to be hard-working and patient – but there is a price for every trait. You could say: "It's rubbish that this thing has happened to me," or you could say: "This is the price you pay for a trait which is resilience."'

Success, in the form of recovery, of being able to walk again and then gaining a first through all these travails was an enormous achievement, instrumental in forging Buscombe's character. 'You realize as you grow up that there will not always be somebody there telling you that you will be good enough and you have to find your own inner confidence,' she says. 'That was a big part of my life, learning that you don't gain confidence by saying affirmations in a mirror but by having a stack of undeniable proof that you are what you say you are, that you have to work out your self-doubt.'

She went on to take a Master's at Cambridge and it too proved to be a turning point. Her thesis studied the use of DRS (the Drag Reduction System used by drivers to gain speed and assist in overtaking), overseen by the former Jaguar team principal Tony Purnell and working with the FIA and the then F1 race director Charlie Whiting. Her work on DRS also led to a revelation, that her interest in the system was less about the aerodynamic specification of the DRS flap itself but more about the nature of racing.

'That's how I got bitten by the strategy bug,' she says. 'I realized it was really rather cool, and it was the same maths as poker or high-speed chess. I liked the gamesmanship of it and from then on I wanted to work in strategy.'

Buscombe applied for every job available in F1 but it was eventually Ferrari that came to her. She had worked with the Scuderia on her thesis and was offered a job in simulator development. For a lifelong McLaren fan this had not been the plan. She likens her feelings before going to the interview as akin to visiting the Death Star, such was her allegiance to McLaren, but was unprepared for quite how entranced she would be by Ferrari's factory at Maranello.

'I just fell in love with it. There was some prancing horse magic happening in my soul,' she recalls. 'Ferrari is different.

I don't know how else to describe it other than it is a bit of racing Disneyland. The old race bays, seeing the heritage and feeling it, it struck a nerve in my soul that I didn't even know existed.'

After finally admitting she had joined the dark side to her McLaren-loving father, Buscombe gave her all with Ferrari in sim development but her heart remained set on strategy, so she began volunteering to work with the Ferrari strategists at weekends. One in particular, the US Grand Prix in 2012, cemented her love for the role.

Ferrari needed third place to keep Fernando Alonso in the title fight, but he and teammate Felipe Massa had both qualified on the dirty side of the grid. With the startline disadvantage at Austin from that side enormous, the team desperately searched for answers. Buscombe and her co-workers came up with the idea of breaking the post-qualifying gearbox seal on Massa's car, giving him a three-place penalty, which moved both drivers to the clean side of the grid. A simple but inspired piece of strategic thinking and it worked.

'It was a piece of maths that started on a napkin,' she says. 'But it ended up being enough, we got to P3 and the championship was kept alive for another day.'

Ferrari acknowledged her skill and she was promoted to be Massa's car-based race strategist the following year, still working remotely from Maranello. She then took a step up in 2016 as full strategy engineer with Haas, the first time she was attending all the races making the calls from the pit wall. With Haas a considerably smaller operation than the Scuderia, she was in at the deep end, the only person calling strategy at the team without the enormous back-up staff enjoyed at Ferrari.

Once more it was a learning experience and having proved herself more than capable, Buscombe was poached by Sauber (the team which would become Alfa Romeo in 2019) midway through the season to become their head of race strategy. It was another baptism of fire. The team was underperforming at the time and in a dogfight for tenth place in the championship with the now defunct Manor team. Once more it was a character-forging moment, if one that probably went largely unnoticed at the back of the field.

'Some of the battles we had were truly excellent. We were three seconds off the pace but the racing was fantastic,' she says. 'It was such good strategy, two laps down from the race leaders, but if you look back on some of the strategies then, look at some of the tricks we did then, we are still using them now.'

It worked too, as the team's strategy in Brazil ensured Felipe Nasr took ninth and with it tenth in the championship. It was a turning point for the team as it began to show a real improvement from the following season.

Buscombe's role itself is complex to the point of perhaps almost being impenetrable, but for someone for whom numbers have always danced, one to which she is well suited. The sharp end might be on Sunday but so much of the work is in the preparation.

She describes the team of strategists as working on 'storytelling'. They run through as many scenarios as possible of what they think the race will look like. Then they consider the introduction of variables: when tyre degradation is higher than expected, requiring an extra stop; the alternatives if a safety car is deployed; or in case of weather changes.

These alternative timelines and plans are given alphabetical designations and Buscombe helpfully clears up the popular misconception that the most favoured option is plan A.

'We will build a storybook, which we then present to the drivers, and we will come up with plans and give them names,' she says. 'So for comms, everybody is clear going into the race which is plan A, plan B, plan C. They might not even be in order, as plan C might be the thing you really want to do.'

The strategist's role then is to make the best possible decisions across a full race weekend to facilitate the best result. As the week builds up it will begin with decisions on tyre usage, how many and when to use them in practice according to what might be needed in qualifying and the race itself. However for all plans, data collection is vital, with one session at practice usually given over to allow strategists to build up the knowledge they need about the track, the options it presents and to feed into their estimates of competitiveness. The strategists then, in turn, feed back to race engineers to help them optimize set-up for the proposed alternative run plans.

In qualifying this translates into relatively straightforward decisions where timing is key – when to send the car out, how many runs are needed to optimize performance – but on race day the process ramps up to a crescendo.

'On the pit wall you have to approach it as though you were flying a fighter plane or you were in space,' explains Buscombe. 'In that you have procedures in place, so you can react when something bad happens or something unexpected happens. So we have procedures, plans in place so that even if it's not the exact permutation of a scenario you have looked at, you know you can adapt from a procedure you have in hand.'

To this end communication is key. The strategist will draw on information from the driver of course, but also from weather watchers, from tyre experts, the onboard data experts, other strategists updating their pre-race models, even competitors' radio messages, all feeding in to making a live decision which is always against the clock.

It sounds impossibly tense and it is, but as Buscombe notes: 'Panicking is the only real mistake.' Even with so many variables of possibilities modelled, the reality is often very fluid. The military maxim that 'no plan survives contact with the enemy' seems as applicable here as on the battlefield.

'You might not see a car as a concern but then they have a mega start and that all suddenly changes,' says Buscombe. 'You are always reacting to positions, trying to tune your predictions as the race unfolds so you can build a projection of what you think the race will look like and the better projections you have got, the better job you can do. What it comes down to is a big mathletes competition, where you have to do a better job than the other guys.'

Nor, it should be noted, is the goal necessarily simply to be aiming at the highest finishing position. Sometimes it is about maximizing with a view of the bigger picture. In 2022 with Alfa Romeo in a tight fight with Aston Martin for sixth place, by the time they reached the final two rounds in Brazil and Abu Dhabi the strategy was geared around beating Aston. In Brazil, an aggressive strategy with an undercut paid off, securing Valtteri Bottas ninth place and the two points that advanced Alfa to sixth. It was a consummate piece of strategy, executed to perfection, as it had to be to put Bottas out in front of Sebastian Vettel.

At the next round in Abu Dhabi, however, without the pace for points, the drivers were tasked with slowing up Vettel. For the first half of the race it worked and by the close Vettel had too much to do and could not pass Daniel Ricciardo. He finished tenth, by just six-tenths of a second, ensuring Alfa Romeo kept sixth in the championship, a triumph for the strategists on the pit wall and the team.

'That result was so special because it is so rare in F1 that you get your fairy-tale ending,' says Buscombe. 'It's even rarer when every single individual in the team can look at P6 in that championship and say, "I did that." It's all about us as a team, and it was the most special feeling because if one of us had not done a good enough job we would have lost.'

Clearly there is an intense pressure to the task that is addressed by working at improving on every level in between races. Buscombe and the team look at the best way to optimize radio communications, and she studies statistical analysis systems and how they can be adapted into procedures on the pit wall and even addresses her own physical capabilities.

'I have spent a lot of time on my fitness to get my resting heart rate as slow as possible,' she explains. 'So when I am in a decision-making situation and my heart rate spikes, it is lower than it was because there is a point where you start releasing all the adrenaline that can overwhelm your decision-making process. It's something you consistently get better at.'

She has been consistently improving her skill sets and abilities across her career but as one of the few women in such a prominent position in F1 she is also aware she has an influence beyond her role with the team. When we first met in 2017, she told me in typically entertaining and forthright fashion that 'F1 drivers don't care if a woman or a chipmunk calls the shots.' She has not changed her opinion and her belief that gender should not be an issue for the next generation of women looking to enter the sport.

'I am not done. I want to win world championships,' she says. 'But I also like a quote from [Canadian poet] Rupi Kaur who said, "Our work should equip the next generation of women to outdo us in every single field; this is the legacy we will leave behind." That's important. When you are having a really tough day, you might have an eighteen-year-old girl come up to you and say, "I did engineering because of you." Well, those moments really make it worthwhile.

'I have an East End accent, I'm not posh, I'm not fancy and it's important to me that there shouldn't be a preconceived, prescribed route for people, for any people from any background, gender or race. We should try and be a sport where we have the best people and we are as welcoming as possible to as many backgrounds as possible.'

An elevation to princess remains elusive, as indeed does a trip to space. However Buscombe is not only rightly proud of all that she has achieved, but is as thrilled with doing it to this day as she was when ten-year-old Ruth decided that making it to F1 would be the real crowning glory, a career choice she could not be happier with now.

'I have always found peace in knowing that if I want something and I try my hardest and do not get it, I am OK with that. But what I won't accept of myself is not trying,' she says. 'Now I'm here, well, how many people get to do the thing that they love as part of a team? It is unparalleled – and on top of that I get to do maths on a world stage…'

CHAPTER 3

THE DRIVER

LANDO NORRIS
DRIVER - MCLAREN FORMULA 1 TEAM

'When McLaren signed me and I knew I had made it to F1, I was speechless. It still makes me smile even now, that moment in a little office in a truck and I wasn't allowed to tell anyone, not even my mum. It was an incredible feeling then and now, because you have become part of a unique group. It's one of the toughest sports in the world to get to that top level; there are only twenty people who get to be in that position and I was one of them. I was very smiley for a long time.'

Several years on from that moment in 2019, the heartfelt enthusiasm and emotion Lando Norris still feels for it is manifest. There is no affectation of cool for this young man – his gleeful exhilaration at being part of F1 is positively infectious.

He is irrepressibly likeable in conversation, can be both playful and serious, and witty and thoughtful in turns. Besides his obvious talent on track, Norris is extremely good company, and he is honest about his work, his feelings and himself – a trait he knows can lead to trouble but one he refuses to suppress, which makes the McLaren driver one of the most fascinating and popular characters on the F1 grid.

Norris is part of the new generation of F1 drivers – the heirs to Lewis Hamilton, Fernando Alonso and Sebastian Vettel – who are shaping the future of the sport. He may be only twenty-four years old but his competitive edge is every bit as finely honed as the drivers he grew up watching and is typically forthright on what racing means to him. The best drivers are their own harshest critics and whether fighting for first or for fifteenth, there should be no question the commitment remains the same.

'There is a clear competitive side of wanting to be on top, wanting to get the best out of the car every time,' he says. 'We do interviews where I know maybe we finished in a great position but I knew I did a shitty lap so I am still not very happy. What matters to me in the race is the personal satisfaction of doing the best job I could have done. Did I drive as quickly as I can? I am the only one who really knows that at the end of the day.'

F1 drivers are also notoriously cagey about revealing themselves, and there is a conscious desire to avoid exposing weakness which often sits alongside extensive media training to make for bland platitudes in conversation.

Some use this to bat away every enquiry with dreary stock answers, yet others do embrace it, enjoying the connection that comes with interaction, and the chance to perhaps make a point outside the F1 bubble. Hamilton has led the way in this regard, but Norris too is pleasingly forthright.

It transpires then that come race day as the pressure rises and the moment the whole team has been building to all weekend looms, Norris, far from being superhuman, still feels the tension just as much as anyone might.

'I get very nervous still,' he admits. 'I struggle to eat on Sunday. I struggle to eat anything,' he says. 'Sometimes I will have a couple of bites of a wrap and that's it. It's not the best way to go into a race but that's all I can do sometimes, I feel a bit nervous, a bit sick.'

The tension is part of the excitement, which he welcomes, albeit he would still like a spot of nosebag before the lights go out. 'That is when I am switched off before the race,' he adds. 'It's a nice feeling in a way but also not a nice feeling because I would *love* to have my lunch but that's just the way it is.'

The concept of being 'switched off' and conversely the ability to snap into race focus is a repeating refrain amongst drivers, of a definitive mental transition that takes place. A psychological setting that is distinct when they enter the competitive sphere is not unusual among athletes. The idea of the 'game face' is long established but it is very pronounced amongst F1 drivers, where 'switching on' is a necessity.

They require a state of fine-tuning, where the acuity of the senses is heightened, where focus is sharpened to an instinctive level, where action and reaction are measured in nanoseconds, a transfer of decision-making to muscle movement that can barely be measured. It requires that any extraneous distractions be banished.

Which can be tricky amid the tumult of F1. The sport is unlike almost any other in that during the period shortly before competition begins, drivers are surrounded by media, guests, celebrities and fans when, having brought their cars to the grid, they are very much part of the show. There are hundreds of people thronging the grid, photographers weave in and out, as do television crews who jostle for attention, their demands insatiable.

Now while a chat with Kylie Minogue, Stormzy or Steve Carell might be a welcome distraction for some, this is nonetheless a demand few athletes must deal with. The dressing room before a football or NFL game, or the first tee at The Open are not, after all, a chance to meet and greet.

Norris explains how dealing with this exceptional scenario involves a duality of character. 'I am very good at going from one face to another. From being on the grid chatting, doing an interview to when I put the visor down,' he says. 'I have always been open and honest in my interviews, which has not always been the best thing, and it bites me sometimes. So I have to switch from being chilled out and open, which is what a lot of people think is what the driver will be like on track, but that is not at all the case.

'I am quite a different person when I get in the car. As soon as the helmet goes on, I am not very happy to speak to people. That's when it is me time, it is me doing my job. When the helmet goes on I am doing the job I am being paid to do. I feel like I am very good at switching from one to another.'

Nor is this concentration, focus and build-up of adrenaline necessarily something that can be simply cast aside after the heat of battle. 'Even to the very final lap of a race, by the time I get back to the paddock it is hard to switch off,' he says. 'To get back to being in the mode to meet people.'

Part of the reason drivers apply this rigid differentiation of their focus is because the stakes could not be higher in this sport where serious injury or death remains an ever-present spectre.

Jules Bianchi was the last driver to die as a result of injuries sustained in an F1 race when he crashed at the Japanese Grand Prix in 2014. F1 no longer has the horrific fatalities of the 1960s and 1970s, but deaths in motorsport remain, including in the same series Norris raced in on his way up the ladder. Since the sport began, drivers have known the dangers, but it is not something they allow to impinge on their judgement in the car for fear of clouding their decision-making ability. Yet without doubt it remains fundamentally dangerous, a reality not so much ignored as compartmentalized.

'We lost Jules, we lost Anthoine Hubert, we lost Dilano van 't Hoff. Things can still happen and these were in races I was in only a few years ago. I was racing the same series and the same cars. You don't realize how close it is until things happen,' Norris says.

But while for the drivers it is a grim but accepted part of the landscape of the sport, it is far worse, he believes, on the long-suffering parents.

'My dad struggles to watch the first laps, and my mum is the same,' he adds. 'When they are in the garage, sometimes my mum has to leave just to get the first lap out of the way then come back in. She has always looked out for me, and she knows how dangerous it is.

'Parents always think like that more than we do as drivers. They think of the worst before the best but I know they are in it with me. My mum always says she is on my shoulder while I am driving. She is always in the car with me.'

It transpires his mother Cisca has long been somewhat concerned about her son's need for speed. He had developed an early interest after watching Valentino Rossi racing in MotoGP on TV and Mum and Dad indulged what they likely believed was a phase he was going through, leading to experiences that have stayed with Norris forever, if clouded with a spot of childhood trauma.

'For my fifth birthday they gave me a little red plastic quad bike and that's one of the earliest memories of my life,' he says. 'I loved it but within a few months they sold it because it was too dangerous. Mum and Dad didn't like seeing me go round corners on two wheels. They didn't tell me – I just came back from school one day and it was gone. There were a lot of tears for several days, because I really loved that bike.'

The distress was perhaps registered and with a surprisingly game approach to punishing themselves, a year later they let the young Norris have a 50cc Yamaha motorbike to ride around in the garden. A trip to the Clay Pigeon kart track in Dorset followed, his first experience of live racing. Inevitably he wanted a go on four wheels and driving a Bambino go-kart proved a game changer.

'That was the kick-starter for everything else, for the rest of my career,' Norris recalls. 'My love for that overtook everything, even my love for bikes. Every day after school I would run home to try and do as much karting as I could.'

Norris smiles, his face animated as he describes these life-changing moments, and his eyes light up as if it were yesterday. The extent of his passion for the sport even at such a young age at this point was irrepressible. On another day at the kart track his dad went to speak to the parents of racers for advice about how to go about competing and a kind soul donated a race suit. Norris was thrilled.

'It was one of those moments when you get something when you are young and you never want to let go of it,' he says. 'I slept in it even though it was smelly and old. The boots were way, way too big but I would wear it all day at home – it was awesome. We still have it because my dad kept it as it was my first-ever race suit.'

As he became older, he went on to compete in karting, but just for fun, and still did not see it as a career. Much as it might be assumed that F1 drivers display their talent from the off, Norris did not win a race in the British Kart Championships until his final year in the Cadet class. He admits anyone watching then would not have witnessed any special talent because, being smaller and lighter than most drivers, he was bullied on track.

Yet he stuck with it until he grew a little bigger, climbed into some decent equipment and started winning. It was another crucial point when he was thirteen years old and his parents asked if he wanted to pursue racing. 'I was still very young but I did want to do it,' he explains. 'That was when it became more serious, a big turning point in the mentality of wanting to go out and win and be the best.'

That was the beginning of the journey to F1. Karting success led to single seaters, and success in F4 followed by Formula

Renault and F3. By 2017 F1 teams were interested and he was in talks with McLaren at sixteen years old. They took him on as a junior and as a simulator driver that year, then a year later as reserve driver he took part in free practice at Spa. Later that season in the back of the Carlin F2 truck in Monza he signed the contract that made him an F1 driver, making his F1 debut for McLaren in 2019.

Norris fitted in well almost immediately, not least because of one trait that he had developed pre-F1 that has stayed with him ever since and which says a lot about his character. He had little to no motor racing background and he was learning as he went, so he threw himself into it.

He had always engaged with the mechanics and engineers, creating personal relationships and getting stuck in helping with building the car, and at the end of the race when others had long departed, stripping it down and derigging the garage.

It is something that he tries to continue despite the demands of F1. 'I love working with the team,' he says. 'I used to always stay and I would pack up with them in 2017 and 2018 when I was the reserve driver. I would travel with the team, help them take everything down on Sunday night, stay until 2 or 3 or 4 a.m. sometimes.'

The number two mechanic on his car, Frazer Burchell, attests to how much Norris still engages with them and cites numerous instances where the driver has used his fame and connections and gone out of his way to arrange tickets for festivals and similar for his crew. Their respect for Norris as a driver is clear but he has also earned their affection, as Burchell notes: 'He only has to be polite to us but Lando always goes much further than that.'

Which is indicative of how distinctive Norris is. Drivers are fiercely competitive and naturally egotistical beasts. They are the *schwerpunkt* of the team, the cutting edge and have an innate confidence in their own infallibility. It is a combination that in many circumstances could make for a disagreeable character at best. Yet those who work closely with Norris have only praise for a rounded young man. He is approachable, friendly and sharing, as his openness about struggles with mental health issues early in his F1 career proved, and has since been championed as an example of inspirational honesty from a high-profile sportsperson.

The McLaren Racing CEO Zak Brown does not hesitate for a moment when asked where he believes Norris's strengths lie and it is not just behind the wheel.

'He is a great team player, great to be around, has a great personality and creates a great vibe in the garage,' Brown says. 'Then as a driver there is his raw talent, his smoothness. He is remarkably fast and never makes mistakes. That is where he is so impressive and when it is game time he delivers, every time.'

Come race week, Brown and the team bring considerable demands to bear on their driver. On Thursday, media, marketing and sponsorship responsibilities tend to fill the day but around which meetings with the team and engineers must be arranged.

These are meetings where decisions are made on how to start the weekend itself, with set-up and with strategy. Plans based on data from the simulator are fine-tuned, upgrades or changes appraised and the structure of the weekend considered. All squeezed into about three hours in between other commitments. It makes for a punishing schedule in which almost every minute at the track is accounted for by press officers wielding complex spreadsheets to corral their charges.

Norris and the chief engineers will also try and walk the track. Once, when he started, it was a chance to get a feel for the circuit but now it is a stroll that presents a quiet moment on a day when the demands outside the cockpit are constant. 'Normally now we use track walks on circuits we know well for not looking at the track, but just to get time away from everyone else,' he says, with a conspiratorial air. 'So we have fewer distractions and we can talk through things.'

On Friday when the serious business begins, every driver feels a sense of release. The demands placed on them by the business side of F1 are replaced by the pleasure of climbing into the car. Norris, however, admits that even for drivers it can take a moment to acclimatize to being back in the saddle, so unique is an F1 car.

'Sometimes it feels a little bit alien getting back in the car if I have been driving a road car a lot,' he says. 'The first lap I get back in a race car is still a bit of a shock to the system. It doesn't take long but it can take one lap to feel like I am driving an F1 car again.'

Friday practice, for all that much is attempted to be read into it, is about testing for the teams and Norris admits he is rarely satisfied with Friday performance, instead focusing on how much can be put into the development of the car for Saturday when everything truly comes alive for the drivers.

While practice is about testing, establishing potential strategies and edging towards the limits, the fine details and set-up changes, qualifying still stands alone as a sporting challenge. The single lap discipline, just driver and track, a pure test they still revel in.

'You get a great feeling that it is about to go down, that it is all or nothing, a different mentality to a race,' Norris says with enthusiasm. 'I enjoy Saturday – I like the one-lap stuff. You get a great sense of competitiveness and you know what you are about to do could make or break your weekend.'

Race day itself, he says, passes remarkably quickly. There are further meetings with engineers, strategists and the team principal and when they are concluded Norris retreats briefly to do some cramming. 'I have all of my notes on all of the plans,' he says. 'So I go back to my room and make sure I can remember it. I don't have the best memory so I have to spend a bit of time to ingrain it in my head.'

The remaining time goes by in a whirl and a relentless ratcheting up of tension. Finally, however, when the visor goes down and the lights go out, every driver is in their element. Norris's love for racing is well documented. He still enjoys the same thrill of simply being 'fully lit' as he puts it as he did when speeding round the garden. The visceral excitement of going wheel to wheel as he describes it is palpable even far away from the cockpit.

Norris has vied in tight competition already with some of the best drivers of the modern generation, including Hamilton, Vettel, Kimi Raikkonen and Alonso, and of his own era, Max Verstappen, Charles Leclerc and George Russell. He has proved himself against them and the desire to have the edge over them in the moment on track is overriding but is not, fascinatingly, what gives him the most satisfaction.

'My biggest motivation in a race and what gives me the greatest pleasure from it all is have I made the team happy,' he says.

Better even than putting a move on Hamilton or Verstappen? Surely not. Yet he is unwavering in insisting that when you see Norris racing, what matters is delivering as part of a team.

'Ninety per cent of my satisfaction, enjoyment and pleasure comes from having made the team happy,' he says. 'When I am on the podium and see the whole team celebrating and loving it, that's my drive; that's the thing that makes me go out and want to do it again. Because they're the ones who work so hard; they are there every day, morning till night; they travel earlier than everyone and leave later than everyone.'

It is a mature perspective, especially from one so young, and refreshing too, but he also places great weight on an equally important relationship with the fans of the sport. Part and parcel of why he has become so popular, particularly among younger fans, is they find an affinity with his easy-going, open nature, his fondness for video games and social media. And Norris reciprocates, emphatic in his insistence that a collective experience is at the very heart of why he goes racing, albeit in a very select club as one of only twenty in the world.

'Imagine it was just me celebrating on my own. That might make you happy for a few seconds when you cross the line,' he says, 'but what makes you continue to celebrate and smile and continue to want to race is the team and the fans. If there was no team and no fans, motorsport would not be the same.'

CHAPTER 4

THE TECHNICAL DIRECTOR

JAMES ALLISON
TECHNICAL DIRECTOR - MERCEDES-AMG PETRONAS F1 TEAM

'When I first saw one of these cars in person and was able to pick up the carbon fibre pieces of them and hold them in my hands, everything was so slender and light it looked perfect to my eye. It's ridiculous saying this because everyone has seen it so much now it is mundane, but the first time I saw it I thought it was magical.'

There is an overwhelming impression that the sense of wonder James Allison experienced when he took his first job in F1 has never quite left him. He speaks in quiet, understated tones but his passion for the sport as he talks about it is unmistakeable, his eyes alive, dancing with the insistent and compelling frequency of a strobe light.

Allison has had a long and hugely successful career in F1 of over thirty years and as technical director at Mercedes heads up a team of people that have designed and built some of the most successful cars in modern F1. He is pleasingly honest, his conversation peppered with wry chuckles, but earnest too, wanting to put to rights some of the popular misconceptions around his work. Not least that the technical director in F1 is a singular artiste, solely responsible for designing the car in a team, a throwback from long in the past he is anxious to dispel.

'There is nothing more irritating than reading someone writing about a car and they say: "The new car penned by ..." and they will pick the technical director's name. It makes all of us gag,' he says with emphasis. 'It's the same in every team. There is a myth that Adrian Newey draws a car. He is an unusual senior technical bod in that he is still drawing bits of the car, but he would admit that it's a massive collaborative effort at Red Bull.

'At Mercedes the idea that the technical director draws stuff makes all of us shudder with the inaccuracy of it and all of the senior folk in this team have the humility to know that it is down to absolutely everyone involved.'

Fifty-six-year-old Allison has come up through the ranks of F1 in a career that began with Benetton in 1991, a team he would later return to. He went on to work for Larrousse,

Renault and Ferrari before joining Mercedes in 2017. He has enjoyed enormous success, at Benetton as an aerodynamic designer during Michael Schumacher's titles in 1994 and 1995, then at Ferrari as a trackside aerodynamicist during their dominant run of six constructors' titles between 1999 and 2004. He returned to Enstone with Renault for their success with Fernando Alonso as deputy technical director when they took their constructors' and drivers' titles in 2005 and 2006.

He went on to take on his first technical director role at Renault in 2009 before returning to Ferrari in the same position in 2013. Mercedes brought him in as technical director between 2017 and 2021 as the team returned four constructors' titles and three drivers' titles. In 2023, after spending some time as the Chief Technical Officer overseeing the team's broader sporting remit including its involvement with the iconic sailing competition, the America's Cup, he resumed his role as F1 technical director.

It has been a quite remarkable career, but Allison is steadfastly modest, preferring to talk about the pleasure and fulfilment it has given him over time rather than the success, that the real satisfaction has been derived very much from the shared experience of working within an F1 team.

'There are so many brilliantly fun people you get to work with, all of whom are dealing with their share of the stress and worry,' he says. 'The sport places in front of you these seemingly impossible hurdles and keeps punching you in the face, but somehow or other if you do the right things together you stay friendly; even when you are all tired and it seems tricky, you do get the car ready and it is done. When it is done to a standard that means your car is the best one it is the most overwhelmingly brilliant feeling of validation and undeniable achievement.'

Allison is also unafraid to admit he has, he believes, been lucky; that serendipity has played a part alongside his obvious talent, not least in his journey to F1, which was not his first career choice.

His father was a pilot in the Royal Air Force and later went on to become the commander in chief of the RAF's Logistics Command, so he grew up as a forces child, moving about as the job demanded from the UK to the USA and Germany. His favourite hobby as a child, as it remains to this day, was making and flying model planes. There was no great interest in F1 in the family, but he took to watching it while at boarding school although then he had no inkling of thinking of working in the sport.

What Allison really wanted to do was follow his father into the RAF as a pilot, but he knew there was a major stumbling block in that he was colour-blind. So keen was the young man, however, he went so far as to trying to cheat his way through the Ishihara colour blindness tests the RAF used.

'I felt I would become a pilot like my dad, despite knowing I was colour-blind and therefore highly unlikely to be accepted,' he says. 'I had a theory I could cheat my way through the tests but it didn't come to pass. I tried, I had a good go at it, trying to work out how the Ishihara test plates work – they are coloured dot plates and they have a sort of logic to them – but I wasn't able to fiddle that.'

With the RAF a non-starter, instead he decided to go to Cambridge University to study engineering, a subject he liked and for which he had a propensity. Having maintained an interest in F1 during this time he slowly began to consider that he might try to enter the sport, enthused by the idea of being at the very cutting edge of something rather than a conventional engineering role in industry.

'There is loads of motorsport but F1 has always had this amazing cachet as being the absolute best that humans can do with a racing car,' he says. 'If I look back now at the sort of stuff they were doing when I was watching as a boy it is laughably crude. In fact if I look at what we were doing three years ago it is laughably crude. It moves on incredibly fast, but in any given year F1 is *the* best you can do with a racing car from an engineering point of view.'

The drivers too had caught his eye and they remain an object of fascination for Allison in their ability to master the exceptional machines he and his teammates deliver.

'My judgement now, and it was my opinion then too, is that F1 drivers are the ultimate driving heroes,' he says. 'As I got older I am still of the opinion that the drivers that end up in F1 are the best, but what caught my eye about it back then was just this belief that I was watching the fastest things that humans could make, driven by the most skilful people on the planet. And when you are a kid, what's not to like about that?'

Having graduated from Cambridge, Allison decided that he wanted to give making it into F1 a shot. He wrote to all the teams and received a reply from Benetton asking him to come in for a chat that led to his first job, but it was a moment he is happy to admit where the stars had aligned in his favour.

'I was surprised because I wrote not expecting to get any answers, expecting that I would probably go off and work in junior formulae and eventually work up some credentials that might get an F1 team to take me seriously,' he explains. 'I felt at the time I was lucky. Looking back on it now, I was even luckier than I imagined. I was qualified, went to a good university, got good results and wrote a suitably charming letter I thought, but mostly I was lucky because my letter happened to land on the doorstep at Benetton a day after they had placed an advert in *Autosport* for a junior designer to work on pit equipment. I had no idea about the ad but my letter appeared to be superhumanly fast. It was the first thing that arrived in their inbox but it was completely disconnected to the ad. I think the fact it was the first caught their eye.'

Further good fortune would follow when post-interview at Benetton, confusion over who had even placed the advert at the team caused some consternation. Allison was called in for a second interview by technical director John Barnard, the man who had introduced the carbon fibre chassis to F1 in 1981 at McLaren that revolutionized the sport and who as a designer returned multiple titles for the team.

It was, as Allison admits, an intimidating face to face with one of the sport's most highly regarded figures. Barnard, however, must have liked what he saw as he stuck with Benetton's commitment to take him on and more importantly brought him into the aerodynamic department rather than on designing pit equipment.

All of which Allison acknowledges could not have worked out better. 'I have a friend in motor racing, a Canadian guy, Dave Scott, whom I worked with at Larrousse and he said quite early on: "You have got horseshoes coming out of your butt," and that's pretty true, I have,' he says with a smile.

A spot of luck but touch too. Allison started his career with a good degree behind him, but also with crucial practical experience in materials, working on drawing boards and in how to use all the tools in a machine shop from working at Dunlop Aviation, who had sponsored him through university. The company made the carbon brakes for the Concorde and he says the time he spent with them gave him a more meaningful grounding in practical engineering than anything he had learned at Cambridge.

Once in the job at Benetton he quickly understood it was a case of soaking up as much as he could from more experienced colleagues.

'Anyone who gets into F1 is taught how to do it by the pals they make in the team,' he says. 'Although you come into it with a detailed, foundational-level knowledge of engineering principles, it is quite a niche business. Not just the lexicon of it but the things you work on are oddball and you pick them up as you go along.'

Which of course begs the question, quite what constitutes 'oddball'? Allison pauses as he considers this, thinking back to when this was all new to him, and it transpires that what he learned about F1 back in 1991 does not seem an awfully long way from what is still the case to this day.

'What was striking was the ludicrous degree to which a team will go to hoover up milliseconds here and milliseconds there,' he says. 'Every single thing you work on hardly seems worth it, but if all of you work on hoovering up those milliseconds for long enough then they accumulate into something that is worth it, but the degree of anal retentiveness necessary to do that is unusual.'

It was here then, at his first gig at Benetton, that Allison felt he was part of creating something very special. 'The care and attention to every F1 piece, where every gram is shaved off the part, when you see these parts they are beautiful things. You can't look at them and not get the sense of how much effort has gone into them,' he says with a genuine affection, an appreciation of these creations almost as mechanical art.

He has played his own part in painting these pictures, works that combine, in the best cases, great aesthetic beauty with extraordinary engineering achievement and still remembers his very first contribution to the canvas.

In 1995 working in the aerodynamics department at Benetton, their Renault engine, which was the class of the field, had an issue with its installation in the car. It was failing in pre-season testing because they discovered the timing belt that ran in front of the engine was overheating and breaking as a result. A solution was needed at short notice, a duct to divert cooling air from the engine cover to the timing belt.

'I think it was just because I happened to be around,' recalls Allison, with typical modesty. 'That was the first time I drew something that the next day was on a car. If you look at the 1995 Benetton on the left-hand side in the junction between the chassis and the engine, you will see a little snorkel-like thing that was cooling that belt and that was mine.'

Having learned so much, come so far since then and spent his entire career focused on F1 cars, Allison remains adamant that the role of technical director is more collaborative than it has ever been. Nonetheless, as a result the job description as he sees it might be less than enticing.

'I'm not the guy who designs the car. Every time I try to

describe my job I think: "I wouldn't want to do that – it sounds really boring,"' he says with a dry wit. 'It is the most interesting, the most thrilling, the most rewarding and even the most fatiguing sometimes sort of job. But if you describe what I do it comes across like, well, wouldn't you rather be an accountant? That would be much more exciting.'

As job descriptions go he has a point. The modern technical director is responsible then for the performance of the car, the safety of the car, the adherence of the car to the regulations and the car coming in on budget because there is a finite amount of money that can be spent on it.

They must choose the right technical team, with the right skills in the right places and then decide how much effort is put out into one area of the car compared to another.

Which sounds, as he suggests, far from the maverick wielding a pencil or mouse with grand strokes of genius as is the popular preconception. But as he makes clear, those days have long gone.

Of course then there is management across these wide responsibilities, but there is more. They must also set the appetite for risk that the team is willing to take. This is where the stakes lie, where some of the real weight of the role falls.

The technical director must consider how brave a design, how brave a route they are willing to choose, for example one that might push down a path with promise of great returns in lap time but with lots of risks before it can be delivered.

Mercedes – who in recent years after the regulation changes of 2022 were found wanting with a design path they later rejected – know only too well how crucial these decisions can be.

'The technical director is really sitting at the apex of the technical tree,' explains Allison. 'They must decide: "No, that's too rich for me. I just don't want to take that much risk." Or: "Come on, folks, we need to push harder here; we are being too conservative." You have to make those judgements.'

He stresses that since the technical director is not designing pieces for the car, that the technical team can be as large as 500 people and there is a delicate balancing act taking place across them all.

There are the demands from the performance side of the team, who look intensely at any way that said performance can be gained, and they must collaborate with what Allison calls the design people who deal in reality. The latter members of the team are conscious of the fact that everything that makes up the car has to be made and used. The two groups must combine to be effective, ideally including people who have a foot in both camps – those seeking lap time potential and those able to bring the grand ambition back to earth.

This is very much a vibrant process as Allison describes. 'We have this group of peers: chief designer, director of vehicle performance, director of aero, director of trackside engineering,' he says. 'They are a cabal of folk who work with one another really closely, really well. They try to bring as many ideas as they can to the table. The chief designer hears their ideas and considers it: "OK, I think we can deliver that but not that." They will argue about it and if they can't come to a conclusion I will say: "I think we should do X rather than Y."'

The whole procedure is driven from vast numbers of the team of smaller groups feeding information into each specialist area on which decisions can be based, the purpose being to draw a harmonious conclusion from disparate directions. All of which occurs at Mercedes whenever possible with an open ease between the departments. 'In our group dynamic they work best when they work informally with each other,' Allison says.

What is also noticeable about this process is how much it has changed since Allison began in the sport. It's indicative of how much F1 as a whole has changed during that period.

'Back in the nineties, the model was that you had a powerful, charismatic, dictatorial figure,' he says. 'Instead of having this sort of collaborative group at the top being fed from the bottom and then encouraging down from the top you just had a person who said: "Today we do this, tomorrow we do that," and would just order people around and then circulate, making sure his word was carried out. F1 now is too big, too complicated and too difficult for a single figure to act in that autocratic manner.'

While Allison downplays his personal role in this complex process, that is not to say it lacks intensity, or indeed excitement. He highlights that the job list he faces each morning is already far beyond what can be achieved in a day, that the guilt at going home feeling more could have been done and that every week and sometimes every day something unexpected will occur that must be dealt with. It is very much a dynamic environment, and everyone must be ready to be adaptable, to bend to the whims and demands of the sporting and engineering deities. A rigidity of approach or an expectation of routine has little to no place in F1.

Allison illustrates how this feels with an intriguing analogy. 'In the film *Men In Black*, the Will Smith character finds out there is an alien spaceship that will destroy the Earth if they don't find some trinket,' he says. 'Well, he is put out by that and asks why they are not telling people and he's told: "There is always an alien ship about to destroy the Earth." F1 is a bit like that – there is always something that feels like it is going to destroy you and the team.'

Aliens notwithstanding, even within this relentless, demanding, pressure-cooker environment, Allison still finds very welcome pleasure in the collegiate atmosphere within a team. His views are clearly shared by many others in F1; indeed it is hard to imagine another sport where this level of cooperation and collective action takes place on such a grand scale.

There may be only two drivers, but the organization behind them numbers in the thousands, and the range and complexity of the tasks they are undertaking means almost every one of them plays a role that could change the game on race day. For Allison, what has been crucial is enjoying his time with those colleagues and it is that, he believes, which has contributed to his success and longevity. Perhaps it's a sort of magic similar to that he felt when he first marvelled at the minutiae of an F1 car.

'The underlying theme that has been constant is that if you are enjoying it and it makes you happy then that rubs off,' he says. 'People like being around you and give you other opportunities. It's not premeditated in that way, it's just looking back on it that seems to be the common thread.

'What is crucial to understand in F1 is that you don't experience it alone. I feel a bit sorry for the drivers as their triumph is a much lonelier triumph than ours. They are part of the team but they are not as part of the team as the folk who have created this thing for them. The bond you feel within the team is tremendous.'

CHAPTER 5

THE CHIEF ENGINEER

PAUL MONAGHAN
CHIEF ENGINEER, CAR ENGINEERING – ORACLE RED BULL RACING

'I don't have a fixed agenda at a race weekend so whatever is about to hit the fan you try to stop, or you move the fan. It evolves weekend by weekend as to what needs most attention, which makes it fun. If we get it perfect, I don't have anything to do, but seeing as we are imperfect, well you don't get a chance to just go for a cup of tea.'

With such a wide remit as chief engineer, Paul Monaghan accepts with a smile that he might be considered troubleshooter-in-chief at Red Bull Racing, with every race weekend presenting a new challenge to which he must adapt. It is a fascinating, mercurial role in which he brings every one of his more than thirty years of experience to bear.

As he notes, if a race meeting goes swimmingly his attention to the cars under his ultimate charge is barely required, but more often than not there is always something to put his mind to, often in periods of great intensity and pressure that can prove decisive.

Monaghan oversees the two race engineers who work closely with the drivers on the cars over the weekend, a role he has previously held himself with no little success. He is then, their sounding board, problem solver and bears the ultimate responsibility for the team having the best-prepared, functioning machinery on track when it matters. An avuncular, smiling character well known in the paddock, he combines a gentle, self-deprecating humour with an ability to turn on a consummate professionalism and willingness to get stuck in if required that is invaluable at the highest level.

He is quietly spoken with an infectious geniality, but also has a thoughtful air, the calculating deliberation of the engineer writ large as he considers what he says with care, including shouldering a responsibility that is broad indeed.

'Fundamentally the car has to be legal, it has to be reliable and it has to be safe, so anything within that remit tends to end up at my door,' he says. 'Then there is anything we need around it to support the race engineers in their pursuits and then any problems we get on the way we have to deal with.'

During the intense competition between Red Bull's Max Verstappen and Mercedes' Lewis Hamilton for the title in 2021, one moment illustrates perfectly Monaghan's ability to address these myriad demands and still deliver a clear, decisive evaluation.

Going into the Saudi Arabian Grand Prix the two drivers were separated by just eight points with two rounds remaining. In qualifying, Verstappen was almost three-tenths up on his final hot lap when he clipped the wall at the last corner. He had lost pole but more worrying for the team was whether he had damaged the gearbox.

Replacing it would have incurred a five-place grid penalty, a potentially calamitous scenario that could give Hamilton a decisive advantage going into the final race in Abu Dhabi. Weighing heavy on the minds at Red Bull was the knowledge that, earlier in the season, Ferrari's Charles Leclerc had endured a similar hit at Monaco but his team believed his car was undamaged. Leclerc made it to the grid only to discover a drive shaft problem that forced him out of the race before it had even begun.

Monaghan stepped up with Red Bull's response. 'We asked everybody: "How do we prove this gearbox is healthy or not?"' he explains. 'We went through physical checks with it, we went through visual checks with it, we went through some start-ups in the garage, then had a look at some aspects to check further and all the evidence said: "We are OK."'

With the title at stake, however, every option had to be assessed. 'Then we had to consider if we put him down five places, where do we go in the championship and someone piped up: "Well, we are done aren't we?" But some people were scared and wanted to change it,' he says.

'That was one of the most challenging times. Something you don't see coming, you have to deal with it at the time and you draw on the fantastic resource at the factory in Milton Keynes. I remember thinking: "I will put my head above the trench and say we keep it." My heart was thumping when that car went to the grid. I was so relieved it behaved itself and it finished the race.'

It had been a pivotal decision. Verstappen finished second to Hamilton and the pair went to the season finale tied on points, a race from which the Dutchman would emerge with his first title.

Managing the intensity of these moments requires a singular mindset, an ability to appreciate the weight, the potential consequences of actions but to analyse them with a glacial cool and it is far from easy.

'You feel the pressure certainly and part of that is probably self-imposed,' admits Monaghan. 'Some of it is the intensity of the atmosphere within the team. As we are getting near the last race, we'd better be ready to rock and roll but does it change any decision? You would hope not.'

His ability to do so has been honed with other similar displays of quick thinking and sharp analysis. In 2012, Sebastian Vettel had a thirteen-point lead over Fernando Alonso going into the season finale in Brazil after another nip-and-tuck fight across the year.

On the opening lap, Vettel was hit by Bruno Senna at turn four, taking considerable damage to the left side of his car and was left rolling backwards down the track, his title hopes apparently dashed. Vettel did manage to make it to the pits where Monaghan was already thinking ahead.

'He came into the pits and I had a camera with me and took pictures of the damage to his car,' he recalls. 'We blew up the picture, printed it and we saw a whacking great dent in the primary exhaust pipe. We knew immediately we needed to keep all the temperature out of that side of the exhaust or we might have a failure. We were discussing setting the fire extinguisher off on it but we didn't know whether the nozzle was in the right place. So we advised Sebastian to adjust the settings in the car to limit the temperature and somehow we got it over the line for the championship.'

Even over a decade later Monaghan sighs, recalling the pressure and the moment they pulled it off. 'Afterwards I thought: "Just breathe, you can breathe now; crikey we have done it; that was lucky." It is satisfying to look back on now but absolutely nerve-wracking at the time.'

Monaghan, as with almost every person who works in the sport, emphasizes that for all that individuals can make a difference it is for nought without an exceptional level of teamwork. On a usual weekend the decision-making in terms of operation of the car is in the hands of the two race engineers. They, in conjunction with the drivers, make the choices on set-up and Monaghan ensures they have the tools to do so, in what is very much a collaborative affair.

Going into a race weekend with confidence at what is expected can often be short-lived. Then when 'reality dawns' as he puts it, thinking on the hoof and working together is invaluable as interpretation of driver feedback and data lead the way in improving performance.

'It works both ways,' he says. 'If the race engineers want something we will try and do it, and if they want something off the wall we will try and accommodate it, if it is feasible. Like wing levels we weren't expecting to try, some fun and games maybe with ride heights, camber angles. Whatever they want to do, whatever gets the most performance out of the car.'

The atmosphere in which all this is conducted, under the scrutiny of the media who can clearly identify if the team are struggling with the car, is a crucial contributor to the success of the process.

'We have a fairly convivial garage; there is not a great sense of hierarchy,' he explains. 'There is a great deal of focus and team camaraderie about getting the most out of the car. We are an open garage, there is a very open debrief, we are a very open team and we are creative and free-thinking.'

'At Singapore in 2022 we had to abandon Max's qualifying lap because he was a bit short of fuel. Max understandably offered his opinions as to our intelligence for doing so, but we explained to him what had gone on, he didn't bat an eyelid about it and was in fine form after the race. It's easier to have team camaraderie when you are winning, but when the chips are down and we had a proper public balls-up, we pulled ourselves together and carried on out the other side, which is a great testament to the team.'

Monaghan himself is gloriously affable as illustrated not least by the fact that absolutely no one calls him Monaghan, or Paul for that matter. Within F1 from a very early point in his career he has simply been 'Pedals'. He picked up the nickname, which has followed him ever since, after he began his first job in the design office at McLaren in November 1990, drawing the pedals for McLaren's Gerhard Berger.

'Mr Berger wasn't a particularly easy customer to

accommodate in the McLaren because he is quite tall,' he recalls with a smile. 'I would design new pedals for him – new shapes and different positions – because he was struggling with the length of the chassis and where his feet were. He wanted to move them around a bit because he struggled for comfort.

'If I was unlucky it was three per race – throttle, brake and clutch – plus a new heel rest, plus a toe rest. If I was lucky it might only be two of the three. I did this for a large chunk of 1991 and the nickname stuck. It was my name on the drawings, and people would say to me: "Well, you fucked that up again because you have had to draw another one ..." So drawing all those pedals, well it stuck with me and has followed me from team to team ever since.'

He embraced it with good grace and still has a palpable conviction as to the significance of those early years of his career. But the fifty-six-year-old believes it was only the start of a journey in which every challenge and new experience is merely an opportunity to learn, to improve and to hone the skills he first set out pursuing when he was still at school.

Monaghan grew up in Stansted, Essex, with no family interest in motor racing but where he cultivated a fascination with cars and the engineering and mechanical prowess they represented. F1 inevitably only encouraged this further when he attended the British Grand Prix at Brands Hatch in 1984, a race with some roll call: Alain Prost and Niki Lauda in the McLarens, Ayrton Senna in the Toleman and Nigel Mansell in the black and gold Lotus among others.

He was instantly hooked. 'It was captivating,' he says. 'The thing that got me then was the noise; you could hear it outside queuing to get in and they were the turbo cars so they were the quieter ones. Then the bewildering speed and a real furore in the crowd; there were drivers being supported, drivers being derided, but it was all good-humoured. It was spellbinding.'

Already interested in cars and engineering, he decided to pursue it as a career which he describes with gentle understatement given how far he would ultimately go. 'I was sticking my toe into a large pond not knowing what I was going to find underneath the water,' he recalls. It was very much a journey into the unknown then, but one in which he is adamant in acknowledging that he was helped along the way.

'I had no thought that I would end up in F1. I just set out to do engineering, and I thought it would be interesting to just see what lies at the other end of that,' he says. 'I was so naive, I didn't know what pathway to walk, but fortunately a few people nudged me on the way and on I went. You rely on so many people for a little nudge along the way.'

Some of these nudges would prove to be life-changing. He studied mechanical engineering, to go into automotive engineering, at what was Hatfield Polytechnic and is now the University of Hertfordshire. Going straight through to take a Master's degree, a stroke of good fortune followed. On a placement at Aston Martin he asked to volunteer on a sports car project they were developing and could not believe his luck when before long he was designing parts for the team and joining them racing at the Le Mans 24 Hours.

The experience only fired up his desire to join a racing team full-time, but after having no luck with applications, Monaghan opted for the offer he had with Jaguar road cars. He had barely started when fate intervened. A belated callback from McLaren's chief designer Neil Oatley came with a job offer from the team, leaving him in a quandary about what to do having already taken the gig with Jaguar.

He went to see the head of department Ken Heap, who had previously worked with the Lotus F1 team. Far from a rollicking, Heap could not have been more enthusiastic and helpful. He described it as a once in a lifetime opportunity and insisted Monaghan seize it, indeed joking that if his newest recruit didn't take the McLaren job, he would have to fire him. It was an emotional moment Monaghan remembers still with a sense of genuine disbelief and affection.

'What a thing for someone to say,' he recalls. 'To just give you the nudge, to give you the chance and you can't say thank you because you are on your way at that point.'

He began as a design engineer at McLaren in 1990 which, as well as providing him with the nickname, was also a source of indispensable experience. Sitting in the design office drawing up plans for parts, the lessons learned there have stuck with him ever since.

'It was daunting and exciting,' he says. 'The manufacturing guys were ruthless with me. They would come up the stairs and say: "Did you draw this?" Screw the drawing up and throw it at you. I thought: "This is quite fun this motor racing stuff." They taught you that the standard you drew stuff to had to be right at the top and you don't expect them to pick up your shortfalls.

'Sometimes the phone would ring and it was car build and I would think: "Uh-oh, here we go," and they would say: "This smells of you; get down here!" and the phone would go down. It makes you very conscientious and very thorough. I used to dread going down to the fab shop sometimes – it was walking into the lions' den knowing you were going to get bitten, but it was the best upbringing I could have had. You learn so much, and they had the patience to put up with me for which I will be eternally grateful.'

Monaghan cites the quality of the people working within the sport as genuinely standing out, the dedication to doing the best possible job they could and the passion with which they pursued it. Traits he recognizes in the teams today, even now that they are four times the size of McLaren back then. He spent seven years in the design office there before moving on to become a trackside data engineer where he worked with David Coulthard.

After a decade with the team he felt like a change and moved to Benetton in 2000 where, as the team became Renault, he took on the new role as race engineer to two drivers who would become world champions, first Jenson Button and then Alonso. He was with the Spaniard for his first win at Hungary in 2003, which he still remembers vividly, not least in recognizing Alonso's extraordinary talent.

'We started off well on Friday, then got slower and slower, and Saturday morning was a proper low point,' he says of the Budapest meeting. 'I looked up at a TV and I saw our car going over the grass and I thought: "What the fuck have I done now?" So we had a rethink, made a couple of changes to the car and Fernando was just on it. At that point you could see the belief in his eyes, and there was no stopping him, absolutely brilliant.'

There were lessons learned there too, from the drivers themselves. 'I was exceptionally lucky to work with Fernando,' he says. 'When he finally hangs up his crash helmet he will be regarded as one of the best of his era; Jenson was brilliant and DC was brilliant too. Not many people are going to get as quick as Mika Häkkinen, yet DC was always close to him, if not ahead.

'You are with them when they are working, you are secretary, friend, lightning conductor, everything. But also you have to give them cold truths. They are driven people so they realize when they have not done their best and each was different, unique and brilliant in their own way. You understand as you do it that there is more for you to learn from each one.'

Hoping for another challenge from an aspiring team, Monaghan joined the ill-fated Midland outfit in 2005 before it fell apart and consequently he leapt at the chance of joining Red Bull at the end of the year when Christian Horner offered him the role of head of race engineering, managing the race engineers and the drivers as a guiding hand.

Now as chief engineer his remit is wider and more esoteric, almost that of a conductor ensuring each part of a hugely complex and multi-faceted orchestra comes together in tune and time as they build to and through a race weekend. How the car that rolls out of the garage is configured is the end result of a sequence of intricate organizational management.

'There is cooperation with the design team, the build team, with aerodynamics to see how we best arrange the car,' he says, 'The design office will have new parts coming to the car, whether a fault fix or new bodywork installation, or to save some weight, or change a part. Aerodynamics and the vehicle dynamics department will have an involvement in what they want to run and we have to be refined in our selection of what we want to do because of the budget cap.

'If we don't all mesh as a bunch of gears we can't race very well. So we try to pull out of everybody what they want, and then we have to try and get it to come together as a car.'

If that proceeds according to plan, track time is the moment of truth. With smooth running, the focus turns to adjustments for improvements, to accommodating the race engineers' requests and attempting to get weight out of the car. If there is then time, Monaghan concedes to going to have a nose at competitors' cars to see what they are up to and whether they are legal.

However, if the car is misbehaving, the attention shifts to sorting out the fundamentals, to solving the issues and attempting to find peak operating performance once more.

He must also carry the responsibility for ensuring the car is legal as required by the rules and subject to FIA inspections. Now a digital process as well as a physical one, it is a case for every team of sailing as close to the wind as possible.

'The FIA checks often throw up some interesting points,' he says, 'We are pretty good at getting ourselves within the legality boxes, it's just how close we dare push to the edges of them. That's always slightly worrying, and I can't help but think: "Crumbs, I hope it's all right."'

There is a discernible satisfaction from Monaghan as he describes these everyday elements of his work, such that it is clear he still derives pleasure from it all; something he feels is enhanced by the nature of it being such a team-orientated competition. He cites Red Bull's first Constructors' Championship win in 2010 as a standout moment of a long career, simply for what it meant to them all as a team.

'The Constructors' Championship is team versus team, so if we can get the team trophy, for me as an engineer within

Above: Damon Hill: 'We all do our bit, but the really hard work is done by the people in this book, who love their jobs and give that little bit extra because they care about doing something well.'

Above: Christian Horner: 'The biggest thing for me is that you have the right spirit and the right desire within the team, then anything is possible.'

Below: Toto Wolff (left) with Lewis Hamilton: 'We have been together for eleven years, we are friends and we are allies.'

Above: Ruth Buscombe: 'I was born with an abundance of determination, sometimes limited by time or sanity, but determination has never been an issue for me. I just don't think I could ever have done an office job.'

Below: Lando Norris: 'When I am on the podium and see the whole team celebrating and loving it, that's my drive; that's the thing that makes me go out and want to do it again. Because they're the ones who work so hard.'

Above: James Allison: 'The sport places in front of you these seemingly impossible hurdles and keeps punching you in the face, but when it is done to a standard that means your car is the best, it is the most overwhelmingly brilliant feeling of validation and undeniable achievement.'

Above: Paul 'Pedals' Monaghan: 'I had no thought that I would end up in F1. I just set out to do engineering, and I thought it would be interesting to see what lies at the other end of that. Fortunately a few people nudged me on the way.'

Left: Tom Stallard: 'It's not about blowing smoke up the driver's arse. Sometimes it's about giving them the hard truths. A massive part of it is helping to manage their psychology. Passing on the key information at the right time.'

Above: Peter Mabon: 'The teams can see all the details from their sensors on the car, but it always helps just to have a bit of a prod with your finger. To feel what is actually happening with the tyre.'

Above: Rupert Manwaring: 'The better you know the person you are working with, the more you know where their sweet spot is in terms of their performance. So sometimes it is a case of making them comfortable, other times you need to push them, give them a little kick up the backside.'

this team it is a fantastic achievement,' he says. 'We have taken on Mercedes, Ferrari, McLaren, Renault, the whole grid and beaten them. Us, a fizzy drink company. Not that that should detract from it, but we are not an automotive giant and we have arrived in their playground and we have won the game.'

After over thirty years then, the pursuit of the perfect weekend remains an ongoing pleasure Monaghan has revelled in since he joined the sport. 'When I started at McLaren it was exciting, captivating and I felt privileged,' he recalls. 'I remember thinking it wasn't real and also "Don't, whatever you do, let go of this dream."'

He has clung on to it ever since, remaining, as he fondly puts it, on a pathway, an elder statesman who is still always learning; F1's consummate engineer who never quits. 'You never stand still because if you do this sport will leave you behind,' he says with a smile. 'You can't leave a stone unturned or F1 will bite you in the arse. So you try to remember the lessons you learned on the way and if you can pass some of that on, then you have done well.'

CHAPTER 6

THE RACE ENGINEER

TOM STALLARD
SENIOR PRINCIPAL RACE ENGINEER – MCLAREN
FORMULA 1 TEAM

'One of the things that feeds back into motor racing from my time as an Olympic rower is that you prepare and you think you have got really good. You do your best and you get kicked in the face. So you prepare again better and you come back even stronger and you get kicked in the face again. Then you go away and think about how not to get kicked in the face. Very often in sport you don't get the result you want, so you lick your wounds and figure out how to improve. Well, in F1 that happens every two weeks.'

Very, very few athletes can claim to have mastered two fields as disparate as reaching the heights of international competition in rowing and then forging an entirely new career in F1 as a race engineer. Tom Stallard's journey then is surely unique and unsurprisingly he has an appropriately fascinating story to tell.

Still only forty-five years old, Stallard has enjoyed what can only be described as a remarkable career already. As a rower, he raced in four editions of the Boat Race for Cambridge, winning twice, before reaching the very pinnacle of the sport, competing in two Olympic Games. He rowed for Great Britain at the Athens Games in 2004 and the Beijing Games in 2008, where he won a silver medal in the men's eight before taking a new path and joining McLaren. He has since carved out a hugely successful career there as a race engineer for, among others, Jenson Button, Carlos Sainz, Daniel Ricciardo and now the enormously talented young Australian Oscar Piastri.

The roles may appear miles apart but as Stallard noted, what he learned from rowing at the top level and the character growth, skill sets and experience that came with it has been invaluable to him in stepping up to become the F1 team member a driver must rely on most when it matters. The insights he brings to the job and the sport itself are fascinating, if some are perhaps a little unexpected.

'One of the things people outside elite sport don't understand is that generally people competing at the very top of sport want everyone else to really hurt,' he says with an honest bluntness. 'Understanding that is the dark side of elite sport is something I have been able to explain to other people I work with and to recognize in drivers. With elite athletes there is normally a dark side somewhere, which is what makes them interesting people.'

There is no arrogance to Stallard as he explains this but rather an earnest honesty, a desire to communicate what is not visible, especially behind the carefully managed smoke and mirrors of F1. He is a thoughtful, considered man, indeed he is so calm and composed it is hard to imagine him at full stretch as an Olympian, bursting with adrenaline, his body being thrashed to the limit, every ounce of energy being explosively released with oar in hand.

Yet while that was very much his task for almost twenty years, now he finds himself at the opposite end of that spectrum, where an uncommon calm is called for. Race engineers, after drivers and team principals, are now some of the most recognizable figures in F1. They are the voices heard on the radio communicating instructions and taking feedback from drivers during a race. They are the conduit from team to driver and at the same time effectively the driver's right-hand man, ally, friend, psychologist and at times a stern, unforgiving taskmaster.

It is, as Stallard observes with some directness, a complex role and far from being a matter of just metaphorically holding their hands. The best must contain and manage the temperament of drivers whose default position when behind the wheel might be aggressive, demanding, egotistical and accusatory with a spot of paranoia, all crammed into a single race.

'It's not about blowing smoke up the driver's arse,' he says. 'Sometimes it's about giving them the hard truths. A massive part of it is helping to manage their psychology. Passing the key information at the right time. So, "Go on, mate, you are doing really well' is always going to sound a bit hollow, but if you can pass concrete information that explains how they are doing and what they need to achieve, it is much more effective.'

In the heat of a race situation there is a vast amount of input and data from a variety of people and teams feeding back into the car and its performance, much of which may need to be transmitted as short, simple instructions to the driver. Stallard will have ten or eleven intercom channels feeding into him. They represent strategists, engineers and mechanics furnishing information on everything from the weather to race strategy, tyre wear, mechanical issues with the car and fuel usage. At McLaren the policy is that all this is condensed into only one consistent voice that goes to the driver.

It is then a balancing act – the need to pass information to the driver but effectively and with minimal intrusion, at what Stallard describes as 'the frequency of distraction'. It means the driver has what he needs but only that, such that he can stay as focused as possible on perfect laps and delivering rather than wondering about the situation around him that he cannot see or control: when to pit, or the gap to another car, or his tyres.

Psychologically in terms of managing his charge in these intense moments of competition and the passing of information, Stallard has drawn on his experience in a boat.

'Our model of perfect rowing was that you were in the zone, in the flow just thinking about the rowing, not thinking about the race,' he explains. 'But if no one talks to you about the race, you end up thinking about the race because you need to know what is going on; that is human. However, if people talk to you too much that is a distraction. So with the drivers I bear that in mind. The ideal race engineering would be to make an input to the driver 10 milliseconds before he thinks of the question …'

At McLaren the team principal Andrea Stella has posited an intriguing perspective of how they should achieve this. 'The visualization that Andrea has while the car is on track is that the race engineer is sitting on the sidepod of the car,' says Stallard.

Difficult to imagine but the principle is recognizable: the race engineer as wingman, observing and ready to intervene when required, a voice in the ear and a metaphorical reassuring hand on the shoulder. Indeed, what is noticeable about race engineers across the grid from Lewis Hamilton's Peter Bonnington at Mercedes, to Max Verstappen's Gianpiero Lambiase (known to all as 'GP') at Red Bull, is the almost preternatural calm and control they exhibit, regardless of how the race is going or whether their driver is hurling his toys out of the pram and has decided to let rip at them with a string of usually undeserved expletives.

This serene comportment, however, is not only a trained skill essential to maintaining the equilibrium by masking the engineer's own emotion, but also another subtle element of the way the cleverest can influence a driver without apparently doing anything.

'One of the reasons race engineers talk calmly is sometimes they are trying to pretend to be calm when they are not,' explains Stallard. 'But when you listen to the good ones, it's also so that you can contrast your voice when things are important. So you can make a big difference between "OK, we are thinking plan A, you are managing the tyres well", to "Maximum pace, box this lap". By managing your voice you can make the driver wake up and listen. A lot of race engineers use that technique to better control a driver's mindset. In any verbal message the paraverbal side is critical.'

Stallard speaks softly but almost everything he says is quite compelling, offering an insight into a world largely kept under wraps within F1. For all that the sport does broadcast radio messages between engineer and driver, their relationship and the methodologies they use are rarely examined. It is a personal, cerebral task of people management and one that evidently can be interpreted differently by different personalities.

Indeed, for Stallard much of his technique may have been informed by his time as an elite athlete but in fact his interest in engineering predates the time he took to elite rowing.

He was born in central London and grew up in Tewin near Welwyn Garden City. His father was an orthopaedic doctor and mother an anaesthetist but for all the medical background there was also motor racing in the family. His uncle, grandad and aunt took part in amateur rally driving, while his uncle also went to school with the co-founder and enormously successful technical director of the Williams team, Patrick Head.

However, rowing was also a family pursuit, with grandad and dad both competing at Cambridge and his mother also enjoying the sport. Both his parents still row to this day. He followed in their footsteps but as a kid also enjoyed watching motor racing on TV and was particularly attracted by the engineering side of the sport. He had grown up with Lego and building model boats and cars; an interest taken to a logical, if larger scale, conclusion when he was given an MOT-failure Mini to work on for his thirteenth birthday.

'I took it apart and didn't know how to put it back together,' he admits with a smile. Eventually a second Mini was purchased, the engine from the first transferred to the second, and by the time he was seventeen, Stallard had a working car that he had built himself. It was a pivotal moment. 'When I was eighteen I decided that a job in motorsport would combine the things I liked,' he says. 'Figuring out how to make stuff and how stuff goes together.'

With that in mind, he went to Cambridge to study engineering but while doing so the rowing also became far more serious. He had taken it up when thirteen at school, where his talent put him into the junior international class and at Cambridge he was placed in the Boat Race crew in his very first year.

In 2001 he was invited to join the British eight just three weeks before he was due to take his finals. He took them but his final course work suffered afterwards as he began commuting to Hammersmith in London for training. Rowing won out over the engineering this time and it cost him a 2:1 degree by just 0.2 per cent. A figure that has clearly stayed with him but with which he is now at peace.

His commitment to rowing paid off when he was selected for the men's eight at the 2004 Athens Olympics. Expectations were high and it was a huge moment for the young athlete, who was to discover how brutal sport can be. In the finals the British boat came ninth. Out of nine.

It was an enormous blow. 'I knew that I had not done very well,' he says. 'But I was also confused because I thought I wanted to go to the Olympics and I did, and so I was trying to process why I felt so hollow, when in theory I had achieved what I thought was my dream.'

As the best athletes do, he learned from it, confronting why he felt so empty in the aftermath, gaining knowledge and experience that informs him to this day, not least in a sharp ability to analyse and deal with difficult outcomes. 'I processed it eventually,' he explains. 'Although I had been to the Olympics, because we had not performed at a level I felt represented my ability I didn't actually really feel like I had been. I felt like I had been as a tourist rather than as a competitor and my ambition was to represent myself at the Olympics rather than just to go.'

After the setback, Stallard found himself at a crossroads. He felt he had unfinished business with the rowing and committed to four more years to make it to the Beijing Games but had decided that would be it and he needed a plan for life out of the boat. A motorsport engineering Master's course at Brunel University was arranged around his training and included a secondment working on the simulator for the West Surrey Racing team and then writing track design software for the company Apex Circuit Design. The firm has worked on tracks around the world including in F1, Miami and Mexico and they still use Stallard's software today.

At Beijing the British eight gave their all but were beaten to the line by Canada. It was another disappointment but Stallard felt it marked the moment to move on.

'No one is ever happy with a silver medal, but it did feel like a properly done Olympics,' he says, 'I was disappointed it hadn't worked out but that was the best boat I had ever rowed in and I felt like I had truly represented my ability. Now I look back and am super proud because when you look at the whole time, the silver was a great outcome from that period.'

There were also very singular experiences from his time rowing that he will clearly never forget. Not least a mental and physical resilience that was extraordinary, especially in those key, intense, pressure moments in the final third when the body feels spent, peripheral vision has gone, as has the ability to even see straight such is the exertion, and there is only overcoming the pain.

'We used to have an analogy for rowing that you are sitting round the dinner table with all your competitors,' he says. 'You take the candle and hold your hand in the flame and the person who holds it in the longest wins. No matter how much it hurts you, you know it hurts the other guy more. That proper, head-banging, hard-core mindset appeals to me. 'Hand in the candle' was one of our motivators. When you are 1,250 metres into a 2,000-metre race and it really hurts, we drew on that. It is hurting us but it is hurting them more and they can't cope with that.

'Rowing is a sport that rewards stubbornness and resilience. Turning up day after day to turn a relatively simple handle with massive focus and dedication. Which suits my mentality quite well. All of the lessons about how you make a great team that I have learned from rowing are very applicable to an F1 team. How to get the best out of people: what I consider my strength in rowing was getting the best out of people.'

When he finally put down the oars, Stallard was already set to embark on his new career. Six weeks before the Games, a friend working at McLaren told him there was a job going as a simulator test engineer. He applied and was told he had the gig at an altitude training camp in Austria. The subsequent turnaround to an entirely new chapter in his life was quick and not a little daunting.

'McLaren offered me a two-week break after the Olympics and there I was two weeks after the Games sitting at my desk in the McLaren Technology Centre wondering where the bloody hell I was,' he says. 'It took a few days to process and I had this moment where I thought, "I don't know anything about engineering. I've not done any engineering. I've no idea what I have let myself in for." I felt completely unprepared. So I went from very relieved about it to massive imposter syndrome and I was quite worried about it.'

The jitters did not last long and he settled in fast. Two years later he was promoted to performance engineer – supporting the race engineer – on Button's car in 2010, where an honest appraisal of his own skills worked well.

'I got on well with Jenson because I came in and I said, "Look, Jenson. I have been here two years; I don't really know what I am talking about,"' he admits with a smile. 'So we will look through the data together and come to a solution together and I think he quite appreciated not being told what to do.'

He was promoted again to be Button's race engineer in 2014 and has remained as race engineer since, but as he learned the role it became clear it was so much more than just being the conduit to the driver in his earpiece.

There is a substantial and wider-ranging responsibility. The task of ensuring the execution of a flawless weekend for the driver lies with the race engineer and that includes preparation. They are responsible for the driver arriving at the meeting ready to go in every way. So the suitable simulator preparation must be arranged for the relevant pre-race discussions with strategists and the vehicle performance department, and then finalizing the proposed set-up of the car so the driver can work with it.

To achieve all this the buck stops with the race engineer, not an expert in everything but someone who must consolidate all the relevant information from the experts in each field: tyres, car set-up, strategists, mechanics, management looking at the bigger picture of both cars and how they interact. Pulling it all together in a coherent way is no easy task.

Each separate group wants their way. The tyre team want one thing to optimize the use of rubber, strategists another, performance might want to test new components at odds with the need for a solid practice and on it goes. The end result is a compromise negotiated by the race engineer that best suits everyone, driver and team.

'We need to get the strategists just enough information to make the right call, the tyre guys just the right information to set up the car to get the best out of the tyres,' Stallard explains. 'But we must also get the driver and the performance engineer enough practice and information to get him driving in the best possible way. All of which happens before and then right across a race weekend.'

Much of this is an information game and over a race weekend that information changes and develops session by session. On Friday in practice there is an enormous amount to process, but by Saturday in qualifying when the cars go out, everything is very much in the driver's hands. Then in the race all this work reaches a crescendo and the race engineer is conducting the orchestra.

As Stallard has already noted, in the pressure-cooker environment of a race, how he wields the baton is vital, causing him to remember a salient example from a colleague and rival.

'There was a moment that struck me with Red Bull,' he says. 'They pitted Max behind some cars and he started complaining: "Why did we have to pit behind these cars?" GP just came back with: "Not enough pace." Really simple and sometimes the hard truth is better. It's not always that you need encouragement, sometimes you need "Shut up and get on with it".

'The genius of that call is that it was information; you can't question that. You didn't have enough pace to gap them so we pitted behind them and now you have to overtake them. It's a hard truth but the key information is there for Max to get his head back in the game. All in just three words with minimum distraction.'

By its nature, then, so much of this relationship comes across as somewhat clinical and restrained, a professional interaction kept within very controlled parameters, but of course it is more. It is all but impossible not to become intensely involved in such an intimate partnership.

'One of the challenges is when they have had a bad day,' Stallard says. 'What you really want to avoid is coming across that you are disappointed in them rather than just disappointed. You are emotional but you need to ensure the driver feels like you are not disappointed in him because you are disappointed in the outcome. You have to manage that and it might not come across publicly but the emotional side is difficult.'

Having already seen out the emotional roller coaster of being an Olympian, Stallard is perhaps better placed than most to cope with these demands. As he considers the two disciplines to which he has dedicated his life, one theme runs through it all as strongly as ever. The impetus he drew on in rowing remains as much of an imperative in racing – a lifelong driving force.

'Whatever you do if you approach it with the mentality that you are going to be the best in the world, the challenge is massive,' he says. 'When I gave up rowing and went to work in F1, I really liked that it was another struggle to be the best in the world. That's my aim, not just to turn up and do a good job, it's to be the best in the world. In that sense the pressure is similar and I thrive on that.'

CHAPTER 7

THE TYRE ENGINEER

PETER MABON
PIRELLI TRACKSIDE ENGINEER

'Over the years, delivery driver, racing driver, tyre fitter, whatever I have done I have tried to do it well. It's not like I bumbled along and didn't give a shit. You have to be like that to be doing what I do now. That's my dad; he always said, "Do it properly, or bugger off."'

Proof positive that for all of F1's relentless quest for technical and engineering advancement, the sport will also always have a place for hands-on experience and knowledge and that is surely embodied by Peter Mabon. He might have left school with no qualifications but now having over a decade embedded with teams as a trackside tyre engineer for Pirelli, F1's tyre manufacturer, Mabon is one of the most respected rubber whisperers in the paddock. Every day he does his dad proud.

Mabon is as genial, warm, witty and self-deprecating a character as you might hope to meet. His conversation is peppered with laughter, a scurrilous edge of non-conformity and wit shaped by his singular path to motorsport's grandest stage. It is a journey that has served him well for while laptops and data analysis may dominate F1 in the modern age, few would argue with Mabon's instinctive and sometimes in the case of the singular art of tyre management, literal touch.

'Yes, the teams can see all the details from their sensors on the car, but it always helps just to have a bit of a prod with your finger. To feel what is *actually* happening with the tyre,' he says with a gentle laugh, as if stating the obvious.

Mabon and his fingers have served the very best in the sport. He joined Pirelli when they became F1's sole tyre supplier at the very beginning of the Italian company's programme in 2011. Pirelli moves its tyre engineers across teams to ensure parity and since then the fifty-five-year-old has been a trackside tyre engineer with Team Lotus, Caterham, Toro Rosso, Red Bull, Mercedes, Racing Point, Aston Martin and has spent the last three years with McLaren. He has been in a pivotal role during race wins and championships for drivers including Lewis Hamilton and Max Verstappen. Not bad for the kid from Fife in Scotland who thought he might not amount to much.

Mabon left school in Kirkcaldy when he was sixteen. He liked playing rugby but the books and blackboard were not his forte; he was just not academic and his current role seemed unthinkable back then. It is impressive and worthy of recognition how far he has come.

'I am confident now I do a good job but it is from quite a long way back,' he says. 'I was quite happy back in those days when I was growing up but I had in the back of my head that I was pretty useless. I just accepted that I was pretty hopeless really because of my schooling.'

Hopeless Mabon might have felt but he was by no means lacking a sense of purpose, a desire to achieve regardless and set about it with admirable exuberance. He went to work first as a delivery driver for photocopy paper and used the money to fund a nascent career in racing, supported by his parents. Always a fan of the sport, he had grown up watching Grands Prix at home and devoured *Autosport* and *Motoring News*. Friends were making money as plasterers and builders but Mabon chose a different course. He purchased a second-hand Formula Ford car and decided to give driving it a shot with the Knockhill circuit only thirty minutes from where he grew up in Burntisland.

He was runner-up in the Scottish Junior Championship in his second season and competed in the prestigious Formula Ford Festival at Brands Hatch. Yet still only in his early twenties, he already felt perhaps his best time had gone. Intriguingly it was an opinion that was disavowed at the time by one of F1's greats.

'I remember bumping into Jackie Stewart at Knockhill, and told him I thought I was too old,' he recalls. 'He thought that was hilarious. He said that he was my age before he even got in a racing car …'

It was not age of course but motorsport's crippling expense that really ended his ambitions. Well, that and a major crash at Copse at Silverstone in 1993. Mabon clipped the inside kerb and went airborne, his car inverted in the air, the driver helpless inside. That was enough. 'I was happy to walk away from it,' he remembers.

F1 could not have been further away, yet the sport's fates had not quite done with Mabon yet. In 1993 he was twenty-four years old and happened to be doing some fitness training with the bike racer Brian Morrison who needed a truckie for his World Superbike Championship campaign. The start of what was to turn into an unlikely but hugely rewarding career Mabon remembers with pleasure.

'The chief engineer referred to my role as "truckie with janitorial duties",' he says chuckling. 'I started that year as a professional racing driver and ended it a World Superbike truckie. But I had a great time with our little travelling band. There was a guy called Terry Rymer, another good bike racer, and we were always racing his truck back so we had some high-speed truck runs across Europe. All very illegal, non-stop back, you couldn't do it now and we shouldn't have done it then. But it was really good fun. Working but doing something really enjoyable with a great group of people, so it didn't really feel like work.'

A job with British tyre company Avon followed, beginning as a fitter and truckie before being promoted as a member of the tyre staff for the support races of the very popular TOCA touring car series, Formula Ford and Vauxhall Junior, for drivers such as Jenson Button, Mark Webber and Dan Wheldon. After a period in the factory at Avon he was once more moved up to a trackside engineering role which proved to be key. His time at the British company, then a very serious player in the market, was invaluable.

'I was learning from the other people there; my experience is all on the job,' he says. As a result I have a very good relationship with Hiroshi Imai at McLaren who is the race engineering director and I feel I know where I am quite well and it is because I have a lot of experience.'

It stood him in good stead when Pirelli were chosen by F1 to become its sole tyre suppliers with the immensely difficult brief of making rubber that would give the requisite grip but also degrade with use to promote pit-stops and varied strategy options. It was a hugely challenging task and not one that has always gone smoothly but Mabon has enjoyed the ride.

Tyre performance in those early days of Pirelli's involvement, reading the degradation, calling when the rubber would, as it became known, 'fall off a cliff', became a vital part of the racing. It is less so today because the drop in performance is not so drastic and sudden, but it is still there and the ability to manage, to plot, to plan around the behaviour of these most integral component parts of the car's performance remains indispensable.

Mabon is typically reticent to overplay his abilities, but with some coaxing agrees he has something of a touch in understanding the crucial contact patch – where tyre hits tarmac – and how it is impacting on the drivability of the car. 'I suppose a lot of it is a dark art,' he says. 'Somebody once told me he has never worked with anyone who can read the tyres like me and say exactly what is happening on the track. Well, you cannot study up on that. You just have to have been looking at a lot of tyres for a lot of years.'

This is experience that cannot be bought or downloaded and when it matters on race day it has been built up over a lifetime and put into practice over a meeting often paying off across bare moments, feeding into split seconds of decision-making.

Those calls made by strategists on the pit wall, 'Box now!' are informed by the efforts Mabon is putting in across a Grand Prix weekend. 'I really do as much work as I can on Friday in free practice,' he says. 'When you hear the driver reporting the car is doing a certain thing or something is happening in a certain way, I hear that. I can see between each run how the tyres are changing.'

This includes as Mabon has described getting hands-on with the product. 'There is normally a "limiting" corner on the tyre,' he says. 'It's normally the front – at Silverstone it's the front left because of all the right-hand corners, so I would always check the front left, see what it's doing. We try and project how that will influence the tyre performance on Sunday. Apparently that is where I am very good. Which sounds pretty simple but that's worth a lot.'

With tyres so integral to performance in F1, each team having an engineer dedicated to liaising with them is essential to maximizing their chances and Mabon makes a point of integrating as well as he can with every different outfit and is proud of having developed an excellent working relationship with them and their drivers.

The ten Pirelli tyre engineers arrive at the track on a Thursday and have a collective briefing with management on expected performances according to each individual circuit and the types of compounds they have brought to each one. 'It used to be a bollocking as well but we don't seem to get many of them any more,' Mabon says, laughingly referring to the tribulations and accusations of teams attempting to cheat around Pirelli's restrictions on the safe tyre pressure usage that dogged their early seasons.

This illustrates well what is a somewhat unique dynamic in F1, with Mabon and his colleagues almost the servant of two masters. A fascinating and somewhat difficult dichotomy to manage.

'We are entrusted with a lot of team information that ideally they wouldn't want you to have,' he says, 'So we are involved with the team but we are employed by Pirelli. What the team want and what the employer wants are not necessarily related: the team want performance from the tyre and Pirelli want integrity and safety and nothing to go wrong, so you are in the middle.'

The engineers consider the tyres in terms of the specific compound of which they are made, designated from C1 to C5, intermediate and full wet, rather than the generic hard, medium and soft descriptors the sport rightly uses for ease of understanding by fans. After practice they will once more brief with data from their base and discuss with the teams what might happen over the weekend, how long the tyre warm-up phase might be, and comparative performance to similar compounds on similar tarmac. It is very much painting a picture: the brush strokes are far from definitive but rather indicative, the hint of what they hope will turn into the masterpiece with an enigmatic smile.

It is also very much a to and fro relationship and Mabon insists that a frank exchange is beneficial for everyone. At McLaren he has built a strong relationship with Imai. That the pair have bonded is unsurprising, with Imai himself previously a practitioner of tyre alchemy at former F1 tyre manufacturer Bridgestone as a development manager for eighteen years.

It is clear then that something of an *esprit de corps* exists amongst all who spend time concerned with eliciting the best out of the mercurial black stuff.

'I will be in the garage as well to see the guys,' says Mabon of a race weekend. 'Because I work closely with the tyre guys, the guys who are actually pressure-checking the tyres, making sure they are in the blankets, that the correct set is brought out to go on the car. I get on quite well with them because most of them know my history and I know what they are trying to do and that it is pretty hard work.'

Pre-running in the weekend, Pirelli will also conduct track-specific tests, one known with pleasing bluntness as 'tarmac roughness', a laser scan of the surface that measures and indicates what its abrasion rate might be. It has now been joined by a new piece of kit assessing grip using a small go-kart tyre, a work in progress that measures the resistance on the track. Data gathered then helps predict tyre performance having been fed back to the modelling department at Pirelli's headquarters in Milan and in turn passed to the teams.

Mabon was key in refining the roughness test. 'I did tarmac roughness procedure for ten years,' he says. 'I set up the laser scanning machine. My legacy was doing that. The current kit is the third or fourth iteration; the stuff now was all my input in the kit they are using.'

Tests done, on Friday what is generally a fifteen-hour day sees the tyre engineers with the teams monitoring and feeding back as practice unfolds; adapting as reality impinges on their predictions from Thursday's theorizing and as the track evolves. After use the tyres are cleaned and assessed each time adding to the wealth of information and allowing Mabon and his colleagues to begin making a judgement on the compounds the teams should be considering for most use at the weekend, how many softer ones to save, for example, as likely being of greatest weight in the race. 'It's a little bit like Goldilocks and her porridge; which one is just right?' he says.

This is also vital for making race-day decisions in the heat of battle and not least assuaging the vocal fears of drivers, peering with concern at the surface of their front wheels and announcing the dreaded 'graining' is occurring. This is a process of the tyre degrading and abrading rubber and then with the intense heat, re-fusing with those pieces of rubber, creating ridges rather than a flat, smooth, contact patch with the track.

Yet it is not always quite the calamity drivers indicate over team radio as they busily inform the pit wall of their fears; tyres can work through it and once more find their feet.

'When we have graining, if it's when the front tyres look like icing sugar on a Christmas cake then it's not working properly,' says Mabon. 'But you need to know if you think it is going to be big limitation or not. Graining or abrasion might be there but it might not slow you down. So you need to feed back on that. There's no point in going on about graining if the car's not going to get any slower. Drivers might see it and tell the team but they can tell them you have double-checked and don't worry about it.'

The process of observing temperatures, performance, graining and blistering all transfers back and forth between team and engineer, building a picture of how much a driver and set-up can influence. The rears might be getting hot in practice, causing concern for team analysts at the factory but experienced tyre engineers can make the call whether it is going to affect performance and give the go-ahead to push on, potentially crucial come race day.

Qualifying on Saturday similarly is a matter of observation and trying to advise, adapting to a rapidly evolving track as the rubber laid down enhances the grip. 'Quali is like a firework and once Q1 starts, it's pretty quick and relentless. You can normally feel the tyres getting more and more tacky, getting stickier and stickier,' says Mabon. 'At the start of quali the tyres don't feel all that sticky; if you get them working to the end of Q2 I can feed back that I can feel the stickiness of the tyres.'

With all the data, predictions and observations made, come Sunday it is the live reaction that matters. Once the race starts, Mabon and his colleagues are looking to the first pit-stops. Their judgement is swift.

'When there is a pit-stop, within four laps we have fully checked the tyres,' he says. 'They have been scraped and cleaned up so we can check them for wear and all of that information is back with the team and they have the full prediction on any graining, overheating or blistering. All of that is back with them within four laps.

'That's why the guy who stops first is like a guinea pig and the second stint can be extended quite long; that's because of the information supplied on that first pit-stop.'

Said information can change the course of a race, especially one where tyre strategy has proved vital. As Verstappen demonstrated in his debut F1 win at Barcelona in 2016, a mighty piece of racing and rubber management to hold off Kimi Raikkonen, when Mabon was working with Verstappen's Red Bull team.

Yet much as the stops might seem the weekend is finally over in terms of tyres, Mabon's dedication and commitment cannot be switched off. 'Once the pit-stops are done, that's pretty much it for me. But as I tell the team: "I am an extra pair of legs as well,"' he says. 'So I will keep an eye on things like the wind direction and stuff like that. It's amazing how many times the teams don't notice when they are looking at weather on laptops that the wind has changed direction. That can often contribute to the car locking up or a flat spot or the driver making a mistake, daft things like that.'

Nor should his nose for such things be sniffed at. At Melbourne in 2019 he was credited with putting Valtteri Bottas on pole. 'Mercedes told me: "That pole position is definitely yours." The wind changed direction during Q3 and I told them. They did a flap adjust between the runs and they reckon that me noticing that wind changing direction had put them on pole.'

With so much experience, Mabon has also had plenty of time to reflect on just where a driver can make a difference to all his and Pirelli's analysis and data. 'Lewis was definitely very good with his tyres,' he says of the British multiple world champion, noting that innate skill sometimes defies any amount of predictions or analysis. As Hamilton proved in Turkey in 2020 as he took a remarkable seventh championship by literally driving the grooves off his wet tyres to a win. 'Some of it is just not so much looking after the tyres, it's just that he has so much ability he is not trying very hard,' Mabon observes.

He also recognizes and appreciates Hamilton's rival Verstappen as a tyre wrangler of great accomplishment. Not least in his stunning drive at Brazil in 2016, coming back from sixteenth to third in the rain at Interlagos. 'Max was at Red Bull when I was there. I had the great fortune to be the tyre engineer in Barcelona when Max appeared and won the damn thing,' he says.

'I was taken with him straight away that he was just quite polite. I know he can come over as being not that pleasant but he will still smile at me in the paddock. That time in Brazil when it was wet, he looked like a superstar. It was red-flagged and Gianpiero Lambiase, his race engineer, said to me, "Can you have a word with him? I can't get through to him because he is taking too many risks." So I had a chat with him and he was just laughing and he said, "Honestly, I am not pushing. I don't know why everybody is going so slowly."'

Mabon clearly enjoys the fond memory. He has many from a life shared with wife and children but one where he never dreamed F1 would end up defining his career from such humble beginnings. He is an inspiration in how doing it properly wins out over buggering off.

'I am aware I am one of only ten on the planet. There are only ten F1 tyre engineers and that makes me happy,' he says with quiet and justified pride. 'I am quite proud of it really; none of it was planned. To be working in F1 does seem quite ridiculous. I have gone from one thing to the next but what is fantastic is when you are there with the teams; I have always said it feels like a real privilege to be there with them.'

CHAPTER 8

THE PERFORMANCE COACH

RUPERT MANWARING
PERFORMANCE COACH - SCUDERIA FERRARI

'Working so closely with a driver, their right-hand man, you become a weird hybrid of friend, confidant and colleague. You know them well, so seeing them in the heat of battle you know where it is they perform at their best mentally. So you try and nudge them into that space, where they are confident but also aware and in a sweet spot of high performance. How? Well, it's a little bit of carrot and stick ...'

Very few in F1 can lay claim to sharing such a close, personal relationship with a driver as their performance coach. Once unheard of in F1, they are now an essential weapon in any driver's arsenal. Trainer, physio, nutritionist, sounding board and perhaps most importantly the psychological tactician on which many competitors depend. In a sport where so much weight is carried on an individual's shoulders, they forge a remarkable and perhaps unique connection with the men at the sharp end, as Rupert Manwaring has built with his eight years alongside Ferrari's Carlos Sainz.

That Manwaring enjoys his role is palpable. The thirty-nine-year-old clearly adores being in F1, his enthusiasm and humour matched by a genuine passion for the sport and his place in it that are the measure of why he has proved so successful in what is the very definition of F1's 'people person' position, and who will, in 2024, become performance coach for world champion Max Verstappen.

That the relationship between performance coach and driver must be one of mutual trust and respect is manifest, but there must also be a personal connection and drivers with experience will generally choose their own coach, employ them themselves and take them with them when they switch between teams.

Manwaring was born in Redhill in Surrey but grew up all over the country as his father, who also worked in F1, moved between teams. He first met Sainz in 2016 when the Spaniard was entering his second season in F1 at Toro Rosso. The pair have been together ever since, with the British performance coach going with Sainz to Renault, McLaren and ultimately to one of the greatest seats in racing at Ferrari. He felt that they would work well together from the off.

'We met at Carluccio's on Fulham Road,' he says with a smile of the first time he encountered the man who was to come with fondness to call him 'Ruperto'. 'Carlos had a flat round the corner and it was clear he was a lovely guy. We got on very well. We were both 'juniors' – he is Carlos Sainz Jr, I am Rupert Manwaring Jr. Both our fathers had been in motorsport and we had both grown up with it so we had similarities and got on very well.

'He was a really, really nice guy, very thoughtful, very considerate and also very enthusiastic, passionate about motorsport and you could see he had a deep desire to succeed. When we met over coffee, you could see the desire, but until I started working with him closely I didn't know quite how competitive he was.'

Manwaring acknowledges he too is highly competitive and was then most impressed when they left coffee in Fulham behind and got to work, witnessing a driver he felt would leave no stone unturned in his determination to pursue his ambition of becoming a world champion.

'I know every driver says they want to be world champion but it was how he said it, so convincingly; it was like something had switched in his head; it was like the cool, calm, chatty, fun-loving guy switched off,' he says. 'His desire, his work ethic was there to back up what he wanted to achieve. I saw it at the first race, seeing how he prepares, seeing how focused he is just before he jumps in the car, and how everything else is locked out. We had gone from that nice, friendly coffee to seeing just how something in him switched and he was a different beast altogether and that's when I understood how much of a fighter, how much of a competitive beast he is.'

Admiring Sainz's commitment, Manwaring has thrown himself wholeheartedly into supporting his man ever since. Yet this was a role that he came to almost by chance, and certainly fate played its part. Manwaring's father was a draughtsman who wanted to work in F1 and in 1977 managed to persuade John Surtees to give him a job with his team. From there he moved on to being assistant team manager for Brabham in their glory years of the early 1980s, working with F1's illuminati of the time, Bernie Ecclestone, Herbie Blash, Charlie Whiting and Gordon Murray. He moved on to Team Lotus, Tyrrell and Minardi as team manager and Manwaring Jr followed him as he went. Yet much as the youngster enjoyed F1, he did not expect to work in it.

'I like team sports, human sports, ones that don't involve too much technology. We used to go to Silverstone every year. Maybe one or two other races and I was always interested in the human side of it. When I was younger I really got into it but there was nothing that suited my skill set, so I was looking at the communications side.'

He duly flirted with journalism before deciding on going into sports science at university: the study of physiology, biomechanics and psychology.

'I was interested in the physical side of working with athletes,' he says. 'I wanted to work with athletes in a coaching capacity, on the performance or rehab side. The idea of working with athletes really appealed.'

He went on to work for Nuffield Health with the bank Goldman Sachs as a health physiologist and doing freelance work with boxer Derek Chisora, London Scottish rugby club and on cycling sportives, pro-am events in France and in

Italy. Yet he had also retained that interest in motor racing. While studying for an MSc in 2012 he decided to indulge his previous passion and use some of the university's equipment to measure the heart rate and physiological responses of racing drivers while competing.

'I had started to hear about this physio or performance coach type role that drivers were having,' he says. 'I got interested in that. There was very little research in sports science on motor racing drivers. The stress response had not been hugely measured, so I thought I could measure it with this gear.'

Having duly done so successfully with willing sports car drivers, Manwaring had, in the process, formed relationships with teams and drivers to the extent that he began working with a range of sports car outfits in endurance races including the Le Mans and Daytona 24 Hours.

'I was the team therapist, to manage the drivers' time when they are out of the car, make sure they get the right food, right drink, deal with any aches or pains with sports massage or treatment and you make a sleep plan or a rest plan,' he says. 'I was learning as I did it, based on what I knew of sports science and sports massage, of injury and recovery. Everything I learned I was applying to the real motor racing world. I was teaching them and coaching them but I was learning too, and because you are looking after more than one driver, your exposure to different approaches increases and your learning accelerates.'

In 2014 the idea of the performance coach was gaining traction, with some making an impression beyond their role. Mike Collier was world champion Jenson Button's trainer for almost a decade. He became well known and recognizable as

'Mikey Muscles', the performance coach always at Button's side who would also play a role in bringing Manwaring and Sainz together.

Manwaring was considering his future during a pit lane walkabout at Silverstone when he spotted Collier. 'I saw Mike and I debated whether to speak to him or not. I was a bit shy but went for it,' he explains. 'I made a fumbled attempt to introduce myself and explain why I was disturbing him. I said I was interested in his role and asked if I could talk to him about it. He was super friendly and said not a problem. I was pretty chuffed with myself.'

The pair duly conversed and Collier put Manwaring on to the Hintsa sports performance group who place a lot of physios and coaches with drivers. Angela Cullen was at Hintsa and in 2016 was paired with Lewis Hamilton as his performance coach, working with him until 2023 during which time the pair formed such a close bond that Hamilton described her as 'one of the greatest things that's happened to me in my life'.

Hintsa assessed Manwaring's work and, clearly spotting potential, with no little alacrity offered him that chance to meet Sainz who needed a coach. It was, it seems, fated to happen.

Manwaring tells a wonderful tale of meeting his former client Chisora. The boxer, sitting in his car at traffic lights, spotted the coach walking down the street carrying a massage table. 'Derek shouts, "Are you a physio?" from his car. "Would you do me?" A random meeting that culminated in working with the boxer for three years at an elite level of sport. The chance encounter with Mikey Muscles was, Manwaring believes, a similar moment of happenstance that went on to shape his career.

'Meeting Mike Collier was a completely random opportune moment,' he says. 'If I hadn't thought to speak to Mike I would never have got that job in F1; it was completely opportunistic, right place, right time.'

The newly christened Ruperto took to the task with verve, first of all with the basics.

In the off season and between races, the performance coach will have a prepared fitness plan for their driver, defined by goals worked out to address general health, but also any specific targets both feel would be beneficial at the time and during the season, frequently with a very focused aim.

'Often between races we will have a few days together to do some quality training relevant for the next race,' he says. 'So for Singapore we would do heat training, if it was Monaco it would be preparation for a street track that is mentally demanding, so maybe indoor karting or physical work relating to the circuit. For Barcelona, sector one is very tough on the neck so some neck training, and for Hungary it would be cardiovascular. We will tailor the training camp to the forthcoming few races.'

On race weekends the task is more complex. The demands on drivers' time are relentless so the performance coach will attend to the details: set up his room, liaise with the team, and take care of his kit and equipment to ensure it is all ready. He will ensure the nutrition plan for the weekend is in place in concert with the kitchen staff. Warm-ups pre-session are also factored in as is potentially a massage on a Friday post-practice. Saturday is intense with a light warm-up but really with a focus on allowing the driver to concentrate solely on his job, to smooth the edges, remove the distractions. This is also the case on Sunday with an added emphasis on nutrition and hydration according to the race location until the final pre-race preparation.

'Pre-race physically you are ticking the boxes: warm up the neck, fire up the vision,' explains Manwaring. 'So some ball games, reaction games, maybe some boxing, throwing balls to them, commands to react, an audio and visual stimulus. You are firing up the body and the mental side of things.'

The latter is key. For a role perceived to be centred on fitness and wellbeing it is instructive as to just what a huge part the performance coach in fact plays in addressing the psychological character of their drivers.

Modern F1 has been long acknowledged as presenting a psychological battle as much as it is technical and physical. Where margins are infinitesimal, anything that can impact on decision-making, reaction and confidence is vital. Putting their man in the right headspace has proved as crucial as nailing down those elusive optimum tyre operating temperatures. Almost everything for the performance coach it seems comes back to that goal.

'Even when doing something on the physical preparation side, you are doing it with a view to improving something on the mental side,' says Manwaring. 'I would look at doing one form of training to improve an output from a physical standpoint, but really I am also thinking: "We are going to do this kind of training because I want to improve his confidence or his mindset" and Carlos will also be thinking along the same lines. I might choose a certain style of training to influence a driver's mental toughness as much as their physical characteristics, for example.

'The mental aspect is involved in everything you do. The real value in this role is the better you know the person you are working with the more you know where their sweet spot is in terms of their performance. So sometimes it is a case of making him comfortable, relaxed, calming things down, giving a sense of perspective. Other times you need to push them, because we all might get complacent and then you need to prod them, give them a little kick up the backside.'

This, it must be observed, is no simple task; it is rather a delicate balancing act, one requiring tact and timing but also honesty and insight. If anything the performance coach must act as a chameleon in their driver management, able to adapt and read circumstances as they attempt to temper the steel of their charge.

'It is hard if they have had a difficult qualifying or a difficult race and have made a mistake. That's not a good time to go and challenge them on their thought process as to what happened,' explains Manwaring. 'It's better to keep things calm and light and once they have had time to calm down and cool off, to then challenge them and ask the difficult questions as to why that might have happened.

'This is the carrot and stick: knowing when to use one method and when to use the other. At race weekend it tends to be a carrot, keep things as calm as possible, but between races that's the time to push them, to challenge them.'

Which raises the issue of just how one puts the difficult questions to the person paying your wages. Again no single solution is applicable. 'I might use humour to take the piss a bit and put a driver in his place,' says Manwaring. 'Young male adults respond quite well to that because it puts things in perspective in quite a quick and sharp way.'

Equally there is also within their remit an element of what bears the hallmarks of an almost clinical mental assessment. During periods of difficulty, one way of addressing it may be as simple as harking back to similar challenges of the past as examples of overcoming adversity – Manwaring cites some of the difficulties Sainz endured at Renault as a period that can be drawn on – but there can also be far more complex, investigative paths to follow. The coach may go over events in a race and question what was going through his driver's mind at the crucial moments, to identify pressures or expectations that may have been in play and whether they may have triggered a wrong response. The role of honesty and trust in this motor racing confessional is clearly vital.

'If I've messed up he will tell me quite bluntly what I have done and that's fine, I appreciate that,' says Manwaring. 'Likewise if I spot something on his side over a weekend that could be better I will try and bring it up in the review meeting we have after a race.'

That all this attention to detail has a practical and genuinely beneficial outcome is undeniable. Manwaring remembers a pattern in 2017 when Sainz's performance dropped off in the second leg of double-header races, so set about analysing why, along with Carlos's manager, who is also his cousin, Carlos Oñoro Sainz. The Spanish driver revealed the second race weekend 'felt like work', rather than the sheer joy of doing what he loves in the first. 'We were trying to figure out why that was,' says Manwaring. '"The second race weekend feels like work," which was fascinating. "The first weekend feels more like fun; it feels like I am doing this because I want to do it," Carlos told me.'

To re-energize Sainz, to return him to that mental plateau of a high, buzzing confidence, they chose to create a more fun and purposeful environment at and away from the track, including diverse training experiences and fun activities whilst on the road. They also involved members of the team in team bonding events. 'We do karting, football, play games, dinner, drinks, whatever. Like a relationship with a girlfriend or a wife, how do you keep it alive?' jokes Manwaring.

Simple enough indeed it seems, but it might have helped. The second race slough was banished. 'Between us we realized that just relaxing, being ourselves and proactive with fun distractions and experiences keeps the environment fresh and exciting and the rest of it then comes more naturally.'

There is then so much of people management to the coach's task, that the straightforward demands of keeping a body in shape seems a bagatelle in comparison, and it appears that while physical fitness can reach a peak and be maintained, mental acuity can always be honed on many levels.

'There is also the team cohesion element, the value of engaging the whole team,' says Manwaring. 'The mechanics, the engineers, the management, the hospitality staff, all the different facets of the team that underpin the performance. We invest a lot in them, not just because it means you get something back because obviously you do, but because it makes the whole experience more fun.'

For all that, with the game face on, F1 drivers could not be more serious – rightly so given the danger inherent in the sport and their commitment to the pursuit of victory – a clever coach will always try and balance it with a light touch.

'What we learned from an early stage was to have as much fun as possible and that sounds a bit unprofessional but it is so important,' says Manwaring. 'You spend so much time on the road with these people and if you engage with them and build a relationship with them that is human and natural and fun, that energy, that humour, that positive vibe can carry you through difficult situations as well.'

The focus is on gearing every facet of the driver to be better prepared to perform at the absolute peak; it is about competition. Unsurprisingly then across the performance coaches in the paddock there is rivalry, inevitably – it is F1 after all – but also Manwaring insists, a camaraderie. They share in the highs and lows that are part of any elite level competition, appreciative of what the tough times cost but also the thrill in success.

When it all goes right, the bond that they have forged with their drivers makes for an almost intimate, personal experience, as when Sainz took his debut win at Silverstone in 2022. When the driver who is colleague, confidant and friend brings it home, to have been there every step of the way is something special.

'Your career often shadows theirs: if they are successful, you are generally being successful, and if they are doing well to all intents and purposes you are doing well,' says Manwaring. 'I feel happiness for him, having shared his frustration, seen how hard he works and knowing him as well as I do. In that moment I am just happy for him and, well, I am happy by association.'

CHAPTER 9

THE AERODYNAMICIST

MARIANNE HINSON
FORMER DEPARTMENT MANAGER, AERODYNAMICS - MCLAREN FORMULA 1 TEAM

'I still enjoy going to the wind tunnel and annoy them by rolling around under the model and putting a bit of plasticine here and there; where there are little screw heads and things, we smooth them over. I love doing that, going to work hands-on at the wind tunnel. And because you have to lie on the floor under the model I always come back with bits of plasticine, silver tape and flow-vis paint in my hair.'

The enthusiasm and infectious sheer *joie de vivre* speaks volumes of Marianne Hinson's passion for her work and is expressive of the enormous pleasure she still derives from the practical business of making F1 cars faster, even after having spent her entire career dedicated to investigating and refining the very singular art of aerodynamics.

It is a task she evidently still revels in, her features dancing with enthusiasm at the thought of mucking in at the business end of her speciality, the importance of which cannot be understated. Hinson is at the cutting edge of the single biggest differentiator across the grid in F1.

Much as there are myriad factors that go into making a successful car, there are none, other than the engine, that play such a vital role in maximizing the pace from a modern F1 car as its aerodynamic performance.

Aerodynamics, known within the sport simply as 'aero' – the flow of air across the car and its impact on downforce and drag and hence grip and speed – has never been more important. It has developed from the simple streamlining of cars in some of racing's earliest models to the impossibly elaborate vortices and flows that swirl around the intricate and devilishly complicated modern front wings.

Hundreds of parts of the current cars are designed with an aero purpose, from the obvious of the front and rear wing and the floor, through elements such as the barge boards, sidepods, diffuser, brake ducts, nose cone, engine cover and airbox, right down to the almost imperceptible items such as an aerofoil on the side-impact structure; a part Hinson remembers with a particular fondness.

'When I started in F1 we had what we called "water wings",'

she recalls with a smile. 'They were the side-impact structure wings in front of the sidepods on the floor with an aerofoil, and I got a particular profile on the end of it. That was my first part on an F1 car. I still remember it and it felt good. I could see it on the telly – to anybody else it didn't look different to the previous iteration, but that was *my* endplate.'

Which may be an apt illustration of much of the aerodynamic task: a series of sometimes barely noticeable but intensely researched developments in the endless quest for extra pace. To get there, there are models, then there is indeed plasticine and paint, but the task is now so crucial and so complex that it covers an enormous number and range of roles. Hinson worked with and across all of them on her journey to becoming the aerodynamic department manager at McLaren, before moving into a consultancy role in a variety of high-performance engineering environments in late 2023. F1's gain, it transpires, was the space race's loss.

The forty-seven-year-old took her first job straight from university with the Jordan team as a junior aerodynamicist and has not looked back since. She has witnessed first-hand the extraordinary development in the battle for aero advantage that has fuelled an arms race in F1. Indeed, her time and experience in working on the scaled-down wind tunnel models has been so extensive she endearingly cannot help still referring to the real thing itself as the 'full-size car'.

'What we used to do when I started out was we had a stick like a garden cane with a little tuft of wool on it,' she recalls. 'We would call it "going fishing", and put the stick through a gap in the wind tunnel wall and then aim the tuft of wool where you wanted it. For example, under the old regs there was a junction on the front wing and there was a vortex there, which was a key flow structure on those cars. You could get your little stick and bit of wool and stick it into the junction and if you got it right you could see the little bit of wool going round and round in the vortex. It wasn't very high tech and we don't do that any more, but in the old days you would use it to track where the vortices were going, to tell you whether your wing was healthy.'

Vortices and this management of airflow is vital but enormously complex. The main aim is to generate downforce, to give the tyres more grip and allow quicker cornering, better acceleration and braking. Yet the very exercise of channelling air on the car to push it into the ground is also slowing it through the drag these elements impart.

Nor does this happen in stable, necessarily optimal conditions. Airflow must be calibrated according to the vagaries of a moving vehicle, adapting to what is happening to it on track. Dipping forward under braking, backward under acceleration, shifting its angles of attack and leaning through corners, all of which make the pursuit of a predictable and quick aero package a Byzantine task.

The elaborate nature of the problem is well illustrated by a popular misconception, as Hinson notes. 'People often picture a smoke wand, with smoke passing over a model in the wind tunnel,' she explains. 'They are great for a very smooth – laminar it's called – flow structure like an aircraft, but the flow around an F1 car is so turbulent that if you take a smoke wand into an F1 wind tunnel, all you will get is a misty wind tunnel very quickly …'

Instead it is, as with so much in the sport, the numbers and the detail in those numbers that matter. It takes a huge team to amass them. The aero department at McLaren numbers just shy of a hundred people. The primary method of aerodynamic advancement begins through computer modelling known as computational fluid dynamics (CFD). CFD uses supercomputers to build mathematical models that simulate realistic full-vehicle aerodynamics to demonstrate the potential of the aero of the car as a whole and individual parts. It was in its infancy when Hinson began in F1 but is now a hugely sophisticated and increasingly prominent tool. However, it is still followed by the acid test of practical experimentation in the wind tunnel.

'What we look at is complex numbers and graphs,' says Hinson. 'You have figures on downforce on the front and rear so you can work out the balance. But also individual figures for the wings and the wheels and for lots of different conditions. Because the model moves during the wind tunnel run according to the conditions it operates under on the racetrack – low ride heights, high ride heights, yaw, roll, steer, lots of forces.'

There is a pleasing practicality and a level of immediacy to being part of this process that appeals to Hinson. 'You see your parts being pre-assembled, then they go on the wind tunnel model and each part will change the geometry of the model in some way,' she explains. 'It might be a different geometry front flap or front brake duct, for example. Then when you are on the wind tunnel shift you work with the model makers, you fit the parts on the model, do the wind tunnel run and look at the data, which is forces, pressures and make a decision on whether that part is going in the right direction aerodynamically, essentially whether it will add performance to the car or not.'

Hinson started at McLaren in 2013 as head of aerodynamics technology, managing the tools the aerodynamicists use, which are so indispensable to their task. In F1 the requirements for these tools are so particular and necessitate being so sensitive and detailed, they are built by teams specifically for the task.

'The tools in the wind tunnel are to make the car as representative as possible of a car moving around a racetrack and also to make sure that you measure as much data as possible,' she says. 'There are a lot of bespoke technologies on a wind tunnel model. They help improve the model, help measure the forces on it, the pressures, but we also have systems that help you measure pressures off-body as well, so in the airflow around the car.

'There are a lot of different systems on the model. It's basically like a massive Meccano set, and it has kit that steers the wheels and that squash the tyres on to the rolling road. All of that technology is bespoke to F1 teams: they design it, invent it and develop it themselves; its mechanical systems, electronic systems, control systems, sensors, tools for measurements and lots and lots of very clever data processing and data visualization. Also we have robot arms and lasers, which is *very* cool.'

As Hinson makes clear, this is a task of immense complexity requiring experts from across a variety of fields. The aerodynamicists are looking at the flow of air around the car using a series of tools beginning with CFD, used to indicate what might be expected and whether they are pursuing the correct path. This in itself requires a sub team who support from the point of view of the computing cluster – the supercomputer, the hardware and the numerical methodology and software processes that make CFD work.

The aerodynamicists then have a goal of what they are trying to achieve in terms of a particular part with a vortex or flow structure and would then examine the flow around that part of the car and come up with a geometry, for example, on the front wing, that they believe will achieve the target. They then work with surface designers who specialize only in designing aerodynamic surfaces and produce very, very high-quality smooth streamlined surfaces, and who would design the new part of the wing.

Their geometry is passed on to top model designers, who have a more mechanical background and who turn the aerodynamic surfaces design into parts for the wind tunnel model, with the McLaren wind tunnel running models at 60 per cent full size. Once the model design is complete it is taken on by model makers who assemble the parts that are usually built in the large rapid prototyping – or 3D printing – department.

Testing is then performed by the wind tunnel team, often working in shifts including night shifts, to deliver the data and feedback on a part. This is supported by a correlation team – aerodynamicists that are more analytical than developmental and who examine the way aerodynamic tools interact – to assess if the part is indeed delivering as had been predicted.

If it is deemed a success, the last stage of the process lies with the aero performance teams who extract the aerodynamic performance at race weekends. Their workplace is the track making sure the team understand how the car is behaving in real life. They have to examine a lot of data from the car in action and also use flow-vis paint to complete the assessment of performance; they are, understandably, known as the experimental group.

It is in microcosm a perfect example of how an F1 team really is a collective whose success is the sum of its parts, something Hinson believes should be publicized.

'That's a hundred people in just the aero department, never mind the rest of the F1 team,' she says. 'What I am always quite passionate about getting out there is how many different kinds of engineering jobs are involved in F1. We work in teams full of all different kinds of engineers and we are working together to solve the problems and do the best job. I'm not sure that gets communicated very well, particularly from a careers point of view.

'We meet people doing A levels who are interested in coming to F1, but they say, "I don't know what kind of engineers there are." I am gutted when I hear that because there are so many different kinds of engineers and we are together, inventing cool stuff. I wish we could get that message out.'

Her career should stand as an example to any budding engineer of following their passion, however unlikely the goal might once have seemed. Hinson was born in Winchester and she showed an early interest in the sport, following her dad – who raced motorbikes and later Caterham sports cars in which he keeps his hand in to this day – to circuits around the UK. 'I enjoyed it,' she says. 'I didn't always like the long schleps out to some windswept racetrack, but it was always good fun when you got there.'

Inevitably she began following F1 and became a big fan of Michael Schumacher, but it was the sport itself that had first captured her imagination, further stirred by one special visit to Silverstone. 'I found the racing exciting and I started to get some inkling of the level of engineering that went on,' she says. 'I liked that combination, of exciting racing, travelling the world and the engineering challenge.

'For my first race I went to Silverstone for the British Grand Prix when I was fifteen. Dad was offered corporate tickets through somebody at work, so for my first ever race we also went there in a helicopter. It is still the one and only time I have ever been in a helicopter. I've been to lots of races since but never any more helicopters. I went up to the fence where the autograph point was and just peered into the paddock. I remember thinking, "I want to be in there one day." But it was just a bit of a dream.'

She wanted to get into F1 then, but understandably had no idea how to get there. 'I knew there were aerodynamicists and I followed aerodynamic developments, but I could not see what the path would be,' she says. 'I thought if my dad wasn't best mates with Eddie Jordan or something then I didn't know how it would happen.'

Nothing if not determined, Hinson nonetheless kept at it. She wrote to teams for advice while pursuing her studies and did receive helpful replies, but was still not convinced as to quite how it might happen, F1 remaining a conundrum and where gaining a place seemed a more rarefied pursuit than even breaking gravity's grasp. So she simply pursued what she liked doing, firmly believing that she should enjoy what she was studying.

'My degree was in physics with astrophysics because I liked space stuff,' she says. 'Somehow space stuff seemed a more accessible career than F1. I just followed the subjects I enjoyed. I'm not sure I even believed F1 was really a possibility at that point.'

However, F1's fates had other ideas, and Hinson's path was to undergo a life-changing moment as she began an astronautics Master's degree at Cranfield University. Meeting the aerodynamics tutor by chance on day one, he mentioned that they had taught one student who had done a thesis on F1 and gone on to join a team. It was enough of a spur for Hinson to leave her rocketing ambitions behind that very moment in favour of going racing instead. 'I literally changed my course that day to aerodynamics,' she recalls, smiling. 'I thought, "Right, that's it then, I am going to do that."'

It was the right move. The Master's degree, including a project with the F1 team British American Racing considering the aerodynamics around a rotating tyre, was completed in 1999 when she received an offer to become a junior aerodynamicist at Jordan. She started there at the end of the year and has never left the sport since. It was the veteran designer and engineer Mike Gascoyne, who has worked with, among others, McLaren, Tyrrell, Renault and Toyota, who gave her that shot.

'It was amazing. I was so excited when I got that letter offering me a job,' she says. 'It was Mike who was the technical director at the time who interviewed me. He was quite scary in the interview, a hard taskmaster, and I still take the piss out of him for it. But when they offered me the job I was so pleased. I remember walking in on the first day and not knowing at all what to expect. Being in a racing team, being part of that was just amazing.'

After two years with Jordan, Hinson moved up to a full aerodynamicist role at Toyota, who were headhunting across the paddock. During five years with the team she progressed to become senior aerodynamicist – a team leader responsible for different areas of the car, the bodywork, floor or wings – whilst still putting in wind tunnel shifts which lasted twelve hours in those days before the limit on wind tunnel time was imposed as part of F1's cost-cutting measures.

After five years with Toyota, Hinson decided to return to the fold at Jordan, then known as Force India, in a senior aero role. She was managing projects, people and processes including coordinating the wind tunnel test programme to ensure that planned parts were ready for the races at which they were needed. This remains part of her role today and it illustrates the fascinating dynamic of the never-ending pull and push between aerodynamicists and the realities of the requirements of going racing.

'If we are building an upgrade package, say a floor and bodywork for a specific race, we know we have to target that event,' she explains. 'The guys from vehicle design and production will have worked backwards from that event to say to us: "You need to release your package for it on this date." We will push right up to that limit and sometimes try and sneak a little bit past that deadline as well, to get as much performance on it as we can. We are always trying to squeeze it. Our job is to get as much performance on it as possible, so we want it in aero for as long as possible.'

After Force India, in 2010 Gascoyne headhunted Hinson for the newly starting Lotus team (named under licence from the original Lotus Group) that would then become the Caterham F1 team. It was a new challenge in starting a squad from scratch, including recruiting people while building the car; an instructive and enjoyable process Hinson insists despite the team's early demise in 2014, but which only prefaced another step up.

Shortly after having her first child, McLaren offered Hinson a new role and she jumped at the chance in 2013 to become head of aerodynamic technology, managing the tools that aerodynamicists use, and later moved on to become the department manager as part of a complex structure.

Above the department manager, the head of aerodynamics leads the department in setting the technical direction, working closely with the car's designers, with the technical director overseeing that department and also collaborating with a chief aerodynamicist to set the aero direction for the car.

This drives the designs and goals set for the aero department, how they are to be achieved and with what parts. Then it is up to the department manager to ensure they have the right people, processes and tools to do so, that they are motivated and happy and able to work as effectively as possible. Having played a part in so many positions within aerodynamics over the course of her career, Hinson is acutely aware of exactly what is required in ensuring a smooth flow in the aero department and it is a task from which she has always derived enormous satisfaction.

Hinson, then, has achieved some remarkable successes within F1 and in a field that when she started out was still almost entirely a male preserve, but her experience as a woman has been a pleasingly positive one that she hopes will inspire others.

'When I started I was very clearly in a massive minority; I was the only girl in the aero department when I began at Jordan,' she says. 'But nobody has ever discouraged me or made me think I couldn't do it. I never felt that. I was a bit of a novelty then probably, but I never felt discouraged or unwelcome.

'Of course twenty years ago you needed to be fairly thick-skinned to all of the banter and I have always been fine with that. I have, once or twice over the years, come up against people who I am pretty sure were sexist and treated me differently, but it's very much in the minority and it's been very rare where they have been in a position to influence my career and hold me back.'

Nor was she shy in dealing with it if necessary. 'If I felt my peers were a bit sexist I would just try to bash it out of them a bit,' she says with the confident laugh of a woman more than willing to stand her ground. 'You just have to get on with it. I wouldn't want any women to be put off coming into the sport as my experience has been very, very good.'

The pursuit of aerodynamic advantage is of course a somewhat endless task. Every year the car is a new prototype, every year the relentless drive to improve, to find an edge, to maximize marginal gains without which the opposition will leave you behind. Yet it is one that has lost none of its appeal for Hinson, after over two decades with the wind, and a sprinkling of plasticine, in her hair.

'After all this time I still take my satisfaction from results on track and knowing we are going in the right direction, but also from seeing the teams of different engineers working together on a project, helping them to solve problems as a team and bringing that to fruition,' she says. 'There are some incredible, very clever engineers here. It's a cliché I know, but I love the people I work with.'

CHAPTER 10

THE MACHINIST

NEIL AMBROSE
COMPUTER NUMERICAL CONTROL MACHINIST - ORACLE RED BULL RACING

'For a young lad from Huddersfield watching F1 on TV and wondering how I would ever get into that job, it was incredible for me to finally fulfil that dream and make it to F1. When I did it was like nothing else. The tightness of tolerances, the technical art of machining components was so out there that it was beyond anything I had ever seen before. It made you look at engineering from a different perspective; it was on a different level.'

F1 is nothing if not exacting in its attention to detail. Neil Ambrose knows this better than most because his job as a computer numerical control machinist, in manufacturing a host of components for the car, requires an accuracy measured down to the thousandth of a millimetre. He and his colleagues, who turn lumps of raw metal into finely sculpted parts, are as vital a cog in the machine of a team as every component they manufacture is to the car. They are rarely seen and even more rarely heard from, but they very much keep the wheels turning.

Ambrose is forty-four years old and having started his F1 career at Ferrari, then the now defunct Caterham, then Force India, is now a CNC machinist, as they are known, at Red Bull Racing, whom he joined in 2015. A team he feels is very much his home. He enjoys the atmosphere at Milton Keynes; the camaraderie and sense of openness promoted among the staff.

'When I first arrived at Red Bull I felt it was a big deal because it was a team that had won four championships,' he says. 'Ferrari was Ferrari and it is special, but coming to Red Bull felt completely different, because of how close everybody was. You could approach people you see walking around like [team principal] Christian Horner or [technical director] Adrian Newey. These are people you watch on television and now I am talking to and working at the same place as them. That was enough to make my head explode.'

A colourful description typical of this amiable and open man, who is forthcoming and enthusiastic in conversation, eager to share the intricate details of a role that rarely enjoys any time in the limelight. Ambrose swiftly pulls up a video he shot on his phone of the scenes in the CNC machine shop at Red Bull when Max Verstappen clinched his first title in 2021.

The machinists with the towering cabinets of their machines in the background are shrieking and bouncing off the walls and each other, and expletives expressing disbelief and joy echo round their workspace, usually a place of studious care and exacting control. There could be no better illustration of what it meant to them. They knew full well it was their victory as much as Verstappen's.

Ambrose has been a mechanical engineer since 1997, and he had already put in years of hands-on graft when in 2010 he entered F1 with Ferrari. He has never looked back since, but that title remains a special moment.

'I get up in the morning and the back creaks a little bit, but I very much still have the passion for it,' he says. 'After coming here in 2015 and going through the hard times with Red Bull of trying to get back to the top of the championship, then being here when we created the RB16B and taking that right down to the final race and Max winning the Drivers' Championship, that was special. That whole season, how we developed that car and were able to bring so much performance, the passion that went into it, everybody believing we could do it and it happened. That was the pinnacle for me. I felt I was a champion too.'

As with many of the roles in F1, the CNC machinist is a complex affair, a collaborative effort, and while for Ambrose it is second nature, his working world operates at the cutting edge of mechanical engineering. At Red Bull's Milton Keynes campus the machine shop occupies its own cavernous room. Within it they manufacture from raw material thousands upon thousands of parts.

These range from the small items such as wheel nuts, through front wing adjusters, the front wings and rear wings themselves, components that sit beneath the car, the uprights that hold the wheel on to the calipers, right up to major elements such as the gearbox housing. They are manufactured from a range of materials including aluminium, steel, titanium and carbon, the material dictated by the component which also prescribes the time they take to manufacture, with some taking up to a full twenty-four hours to be completed.

In the 1960s, '70s and '80s, when what would now be called an F1 factory was often a garage, these garagistas, John Cooper, Colin Chapman, Ken Tyrrell, Frank Williams and the like would be building their parts by hand on individual industrial machines. Today those tools still play a part, with lathes or milling machines operated by a manual machinist used to make specific one-off items, or alterations to an existing part, but technology has long superseded them and the vast majority of parts are in the hands of the CNC machinists.

As the name suggests, they operate very much in tandem with computers and some extraordinarily complex machines capable of carrying out an intricate manufacturing process.

At Red Bull these machines are built by the German industrial machine tool manufacturer DMG Mori. They use the eVo series, with three different-sized machines, designated as the eVo 60, 80 and 210 and they do not come cheap, ranging between £350,000 and £1.9 million each.

They are imposing pieces of kit. The smallest is still an enormous cabinet, in a way resembling an oven the size of a small bathroom, with a clear front such that operations can be observed, while the 210, which has its own walkway surrounding it, runs to the size of several shipping containers. They operate entirely under computer control, which enables them to operate across five different axes simultaneously, moving the tools within the machine in a way that would be impossible for a human operator, as Ambrose notes.

'Forty years ago it would take five or six different machines to make these parts, and now it is just one,' he says. 'Because you have a five-axis machine, it is constantly moving in all different directions, including 360 degrees in the B axis and 360 degrees in the C axis. It is moving in multiple different directions, performing very intricate movements.'

Within these behemoths then, the usual three axes – X, Y and Z: left to right, forward to back and up and down – are supplemented by the B and C axes which are rotational across the other three. This ability to manipulate a component in a multidirectional fashion allows the bespoke tools within the unit to do their work. Said tools can take every shape and form. Depending on the size of the machine, between eighty and 200 tools can be fitted within them. To operate it all effectively requires machine to talk to machine.

'It's automated, the machine is fully closed and a lot of data goes into it,' explains Ambrose. 'Because of the complexity of the movements you would never be able to write the information into the machine so it is programmed from the computer-aided design [CAD] office and sent to the machine. The data is turned into the machine language to control a series of intricate motions and actions.'

This then is part of the collaborative nature of taking a lump of unfashioned metal, known as a 'billet' and transforming it into a gleaming, finely engineered part of an F1 car.

When the design office creates the blueprint for a new part, it is sent to the programmers as a CAD file. A quick turnaround is always key in F1 and every stage is streamlined, so dedicated programmers are used to minimize the time it takes to turn the design into their instructions for the machines.

'They would look at the job and then program it and see the best way to machine it, with advice from us machinists,' says Ambrose. 'We constantly use the machines so we know how best to manufacture the component in the fastest time; what is the quickest process.

'We then set up the machines, and we go about the process of what billets we are going to use and what jobs are going to go on. The machine is then able to do a proof of the job and we have CAD stations by the machines so we can look at the design of the component, and then reference that to what we are machining to make sure the part comes out correct.'

The crucial part before setting the machine about its business lies with the machinists preparing it correctly, especially in using the requisite tools.

'When the programmers program the part, it will involve a lot of tools that have to be implemented into the machine,' he explains. 'The tools have to be built and the correct geometry has to be made on the tools. So we will have a tooling list and a set-up list of how the job is going to be put on the machine and each part demands its own list, depending on the nature of the component.'

This is, certainly for the non-engineer, a somewhat baffling process, but Ambrose takes the bewilderment in good humour and with patience. Effectively he explains each job requires a very specific set of tools, the more complex the job, the greater the variation of implements. Each one has to be selected with great care and the machinists use a tool sheet to set it up.

'At Red Bull we have a tooling system that has all the tools in a crib,' he says. 'We know what cutting tool will go in where and everything is measured precisely against the tool sheet that we are using to set it up. We might have one tool or forty tools that could go inside.'

Nothing is left to chance with the tools, right down to a final check once they are in place. 'We would build all the tools ourselves,' he says. 'When each tool is called to do a part, there are internal lasers within the machine that check the tool is the right diameter just in case you put the wrong sized one in.'

Before anyone hits the start button, however, the machinists, who are solely responsible at this stage, attempt to eliminate any risk. With the data sent to the machine they check it with their own CAD-running PC. They also run what is known as a verifier program, which runs a virtual version of the intended run, to ensure no moving parts will clash within the machine and risk breakages.

When all is prepared, the machine is unleashed on the billet and the elaborate dance of moving parts and raw material begins within this giant robotic Terminator, wielding its tools inside the glass-fronted chest; the metal being manipulated and worked with breathtaking accuracy and a swiftness only achievable by mechanical parts, working to pre-programmed sequence.

'We are talking down to microns, the accuracy of the machines,' says Ambrose. 'Because in F1, especially in manufacturing metal components, they require really tight tolerances. You look at the drawings sent from the designer, and a lot of the work, the size of the parts are tied up to microns. There is a complexity to it so it's not just like a jobbing shop down the road.'

Ambrose knows only too well the difference between simply producing parts and the intensity and precision required in F1, having worked across both fields. Indeed, his childhood dream of making it to F1 might never have been realized at all, he admits, but for being in the right place at the right time. Yet it must be acknowledged that even with a little luck it was his determination and commitment that really made the difference.

He grew up in Huddersfield, West Yorkshire, his father an electrical engineer and his mother a nurse at the same hospital where he was born. Ambrose loved cars from an early age and gravitated towards the fastest ones he could watch, which were inevitably found in F1. He admired Nigel Mansell, Damon Hill, Michael Schumacher, Mika Häkkinen and Lewis Hamilton when he burst on to the scene, but was really drawn into the sport by the then voice of F1, the commentator Murray Walker.

'It was just how enthusiastic Murray was, his excitement and his passion for the sport; it just rubbed off on me,' says Ambrose. 'He made watching the race very enjoyable, he was very knowledgeable and he knew how to really bring the fans into experiencing F1.'

Having decided he was at his best being practical with his hands, Ambrose opted to pursue mechanical engineering, completing a City and Guilds and then Btech qualifications before going to work in manufacturing in Huddersfield in 1997. He did love F1 but embarking on his new career, had not really considered he would ever actually work in it.

Industry at the time in West Yorkshire was in dire straits, however, with companies shutting down and jobs increasingly scarce. When his wife was offered a job in Rugby in 2005, it represented a new start in a new place and one located close to the host of F1 teams located in 'Motorsport Valley', the area near Northampton that hosted, among others, Mercedes, Red Bull, Renault and Williams.

Inevitably, Ambrose wanted to take advantage and ever-enterprising he took his CV around to the teams in person, hoping for a look at their factories at the same time. 'I brought my CV in to Red Bull in 2005,' he says with a smile. 'So somewhere in their archives is an old CV of mine, but I never really thought that many years later I would actually be working at Red Bull. I went to Force India as well, which at the time was Spyker. I just wanted to go and have a look, and it was more about being nosey than my CV really, but I only ever got as far as reception.'

There was no joy with the CVs so he went to work with the industrial manufacturing company Alstom, making turbine blades for power stations, where he remained for five years. By 2009, wanting his career to advance, he was looking to step up to the role of production engineer. The process brought him into contact with Pete Redpath, a contractor with whom Ambrose clicked and who knew a contact at Ferrari who arranged engineering contracts. Redpath put Ambrose's name forward to his friend and before he knew it he was on a three-month contract in CNC engineering at the Scuderia.

'Definitely a bit of luck went with it,' Ambrose says. 'I am a true believer in being in the right place at the right time and that if you're right with people, people are right with you. For whatever reason Pete Redpath didn't have to do what he did, and if it had happened a day later I might have missed that opportunity.'

Despite having two young children, Ambrose's wife Rachel gave him her full backing for him to go, insisting a chance to pursue his dream may never come again. So he set off to Maranello, a special moment for any F1 fan.

'I got there and it was snowing,' he recalls of a moment that will clearly stay with him forever. 'I still have the pictures of when I arrived outside the factory gates. I thought: "I am going to give this a good go." I was thinking of doing right by my family back home and I was high on the work being in Italy at Ferrari, a place I had seen on TV and there I was, with a card that lets me in past the metal gates. It was very exciting.'

The contract was swiftly extended to a year during which time Ambrose revelled in his new task at Ferrari and in Italy, but after which he decided he had to be with his wife and children again. An offer from the Caterham team at the end of 2010 made up his mind. The job was on a permanent contract and sealed Ambrose's conviction that F1 was his future.

After two years with Caterham he switched to Force India in 2012 where he remained until 2015 when he was approached about a shot at a place at Red Bull. Of course he went for it and when taken on there was a very real sense he was completing a journey, albeit one that had seemed entirely unlikely a decade before.

'I told my manager at the time that I had been here years before and handed in my CV and now am sitting in front of you in the deli bar with an F1 car above me suspended from the ceiling,' he recalls. 'That was very surreal. I had made a full circle from handing in my CV. When you think about it you wonder how that was possible.'

Having been with the team ever since, Ambrose still clearly loves the work, and there is a professional pride and a genuine pleasure in the collaborative nature of it that still invigorates him. Not least when F1 puts the pressure on.

'I have been there during those scenarios, sometimes on a weekly basis, where jobs are being redesigned if there has been a failure at the track,' he explains. 'A part might have failed on the Friday and the replacement part has to be there by Saturday morning. So it's designed, sent down to the programming office, then released on to the machine shop, where we go through the process of putting the job on the machine, finishing it and have it sent out and on a plane or driven out that very next day.'

Times like these in particular reinforce how Ambrose feels very much an integral part of what is a collective operation and the connection with his fellow team members. Themes that are common in every outfit on the grid.

'There is enormous pride in it because the onus is on the whole factory,' he adds. 'The departments are working in sync to get that part out to the track, because if it doesn't get there performance is lost. When you know it is out and done what it is supposed to have done, it brings tremendous joy to everybody because it has been a massive team effort.'

Amongst all the F1 teams Ambrose is also notable as one of the small number of Black personnel within the sport where minority ethnic groups are still underrepresented. In 2023, Lewis Hamilton's Hamilton Commission report noted that only 1 per cent of F1 employees are from Black backgrounds.

Ambrose observes that throughout his career there were almost no other Black machinists in or out of F1.

Yet he has never felt it was an impediment or has had a negative impact on his career. Instead noting that he thinks his perseverance mattered more than anything, that it is ability that is assessed first and foremost in F1 and that he hopes his story will inspire others.

'I've not encountered racism in F1,' he says. 'I treat people as I see them and it doesn't matter to me how a person is as long as you can have a conversation and you respect each other; then colour is irrelevant. We all bleed the same blood. It's about your skill set and personality, what you can bring to the table.

'I am hoping that my story gets out to a lot of people and is able to show that this guy is in this book with all these other people so maybe it can encourage others into the sport.'

He certainly deserves to make an impression and is a fine role model who, as we discuss the appeal of F1, rather surprisingly reveals that he had not attended a race in person until he joined Red Bull and was given tickets by the team for the British Grand Prix at Silverstone. Always a special event, when he finally made it to the old airfield, it was an experience perhaps like no other for Ambrose as he took his place in a grandstand with the fans.

'It put me in a different headspace,' he says. 'Because you are at a race where everybody has come to watch the cars and you are standing next to somebody who doesn't realize you have made the parts for those cars. It is hard to comprehend. You think: "A lot of people have come to support the team and see what the team has built and *I* am part of that team. I am the person behind the scenes." It gives you an enormous sense of pride.'

CHAPTER 11

THE HEAD OF COMMS

MATT BISHOP
COMMUNICATIONS DIRECTOR

'I always wondered if it was put on when people win and there is all this hugging. I realized the day Lewis Hamilton won the title in 2008 it is not put on. You just lose it in euphoria, utter euphoria because an F1 team really is a team. Because you are all working together there is real camaraderie, and everybody is the team. When you win, you all win.'

Perhaps the ultimate poacher turned gamekeeper, Matt Bishop has lived out what he considered an impossible childhood dream by working in F1 and moreover has done so on both sides of the fence. He has enjoyed hugely successful careers, first as a journalist and editor of *F1 Racing* magazine, before proving equally adept as director of communications for McLaren and then Aston Martin. Liked and respected across the paddock, Bishop has enjoyed what he acknowledges was the privilege of managing four different world champions – Lewis Hamilton, Jenson Button, Fernando Alonso and Sebastian Vettel – with the latter, intriguingly, the subject of Bishop's efforts to pull off a unique F1 canonization.

The sixty-one-year-old is warm and witty but with a fierce intelligence and sharp, clever, analytical intellect – traits that have been invaluable in dealing with some of the biggest and most fragile egos of F1's driver fraternity and ensured he earned a wealth of experience in the communication director's delicate balancing act of strategically comprehending the bigger picture, of swift thinking and adaptability under pressure and having a deft touch in people management.

On the latter, it is impossible not to notice a pleasing twinkle in his eye as he recalls one method of bending recalcitrant drivers to his will.

'Drivers are the principal asset and I have been very lucky to have managed four world champions,' he says. 'But sometimes you really have to talk to them. I would have them saying, "I don't want to go to that sponsor event; I qualified fourteenth. I am pissed off." So I would say, "OK, there are 200 people from America to see you, flown out by the sponsor. It might for some of them be the greatest day of their life." "Well that's not my problem. I am too upset," they would say.

'To which I would reply, "Do you know what they will do if you don't go? Two hundred of them will tell all their friends. With a hundred friends each that's 20,000 people. And do you know what they will tell them?"' He leans in with a conspiratorial air to deliver the *coup de grâce*. '"They will tell them that you're a cunt." I would say it like that and they would go, "Oh, all right then." It's a bit of an art.'

Bishop joined McLaren in 2008, brought in by team principal Ron Dennis and he stayed there until 2017, during which time he handled among others Hamilton, Button and Alonso. After a stint as communications director for the all-female W Series he joined Aston Martin as chief communications officer in 2021, where he worked with Vettel for two years. He has now launched his own company, Diagonal Communications, an agency focusing on content, PR and strategy within motorsport.

The communications director is a pivot point in F1. The axis between what the team want and what the public perceive. The voracious F1 media is always hungry for stories as are the fans and the teams have their own line they want to expound. There are media commitments then, which are a two-way street as no team is averse to the publicity that comes with interacting with the media. But they also have sponsors and partners to please and the real and seriously time-consuming business of going racing. It is a case of juggling many balls, some of which have lives of their own and often a wilful, capricious nature. The comms director must keep them all in the air, which is why they can often be observed in close proximity to F1's pre-eminent power bases – the team principals and drivers.

It is a task Bishop does not play down and one that is far more complex than is perceived. 'It is much misunderstood,' he says. 'People think it is PR, writing press releases, taking drivers to press conferences, arranging press calls. It is all those things but actually if you do the job right, you should be at the centre of it, as the most strategic position in the team.

'Many people don't think strategically. Many people who are very successful in F1 are tactical opportunists. Bernie Ecclestone, Ron Dennis, they are tactical opportunists; they think they are strategists but they are not. It often makes them much richer than a strategist – seeing the main chance financially – and they are brilliant people, but they are not necessarily strategic. Journalists are and comms people are. If you are a senior person on an F1 team, a strategic thinker and you are utilized properly you can really have a genuinely positive impact.'

He cites the influence he had after joining McLaren in the wake of the Spygate scandal of 2007 as an example of making a real difference on a broad scale over many years. 'I think we did it at McLaren,' he says. 'Taking it from this ostracized, disgraced team that had been given the biggest fine in motorsport history to something that was nice again, respected and perhaps even loved. That was a challenge but fun.'

There is spin involved, of course, as an essential part of any role in public relations. The art of minimizing the bad news, of forging a coherent party line and trying to make it believable. In itself some task, especially given the human element in F1.

At McLaren, he managed Hamilton and Heikki Kovalainen during the former's dramatic world championship victory in 2008. From 2010, he then managed Hamilton and Button as the team vied unsuccessfully with Red Bull for the championship, then through the turbulent time as the team slipped towards the back of the grid during their ill-fated partnership with Honda. It was a testing time during which Bishop's task, not least in handling an increasingly fractious and vocal Alonso, was no mean feat, but one he insists was managed while maintaining a good working relationship with the Spaniard.

Bishop had, as with many of the most interesting characters in the sport, taken an unlikely and intriguing journey to reach that point. He was born in London into a literary family of writers stretching back several generations, but found he was fascinated more by cars than the quill. As a child he would walk the streets of London naming all the models of vehicles he passed.

In the early seventies, however, he had no inkling of F1. It was then an entirely different beast, a niche sport, not on television and barely covered by the mainstream press. However a chance glance at a copy of *Autosport* magazine in a newsagent when he was ten in 1972 changed Bishop's life.

It was Jackie Stewart's Tyrrell on the cover that caught his eye, a car the like of which he had never seen before and he was immediately captivated, subscribing to the magazine and with the fervid passion of the convert, pursued the sport with zeal. Back then the only way to find out the results of a race were in the Monday morning papers, a frustration for young Bishop, who reacted even then by displaying a fearsome determination.

'I couldn't bear waiting for the result until Monday, so I phoned the Reuters international news agency office in London and asked to find out the result of the Grand Prix and somehow they put the kid through to the sports desk; maybe they took pity on me,' he explains with laughter. 'For a year I would ring the same man at Reuters on a Sunday afternoon to find out the result and he came to expect my call.

'Back in '76, '77, '78, the passion was such that I can remember everything: pole position, the times they set, what happened in the race. It was my complete passion. I never thought I would ever possibly work in F1 though.'

Nor did it look likely he would. After A levels he took a job first at a Unigate dairy – so he could tell people he went to uni, he jokes – before moving on to work for a bookmaker at Wembley dog track, which with great happenstance connected him to *Racing Post* journalist Jim Cremin who asked him to write some columns on dog racing for the paper. It turned out Bishop had a touch for it and a stint at *Car* magazine followed, where he once more proved successful such that he caught the eye of Haymarket Publishing.

In 1996 at thirty-three years old, he was made the first full-time editor of *F1 Racing* magazine and he oversaw its golden age, one of unprecedented success in becoming the world's biggest selling and most read F1 magazine. It had begun as a UK-only publication but Bishop's ambition took it to new heights. By the time he left eleven years later it was published in thirty-four languages and on sale in 110 countries. It remains one of the great success stories in magazine publishing and in F1, handled by the kid who used to have to phone Reuters for the results.

'I loved it,' he says. 'I realized I had landed on my feet from a weird start in life which meant I always had imposter syndrome and still do.'

Yet his credentials were beyond reproach and his skills were required in a new field. Towards the end of 2007, McLaren were fined $100 million (still the largest in F1 history) and disqualified from that season's Constructors' Championship for having been found to have illicitly gained technical information from Ferrari – the Spygate scandal. It left the team in disarray as Bishop recalls.

'As editor of *F1 Racing* I had people on the phone saying it was a disgrace, but no reaction or defence from McLaren. I rang Ron and he said words to this effect: "I can't talk about this; it's the end of the world, too terrible," I said, "You are defenceless and you need someone putting your case." At the Turkish Grand Prix he told me I was right and asked me to come to work for him. I liked Ron, a maddening person but a genius, a crazy genius, great qualities. I suddenly realized it then at that moment with epiphanic clarity that he really needs a strategic comms director because he was being fucked by the press.'

Bishop duly took the role that was perhaps the toughest gig in the sport at a team that had only just been able to continue functioning after the fine.

'I remember the tone. Everything about that team when I got there was characterized by what I would describe as defensive pessimism,' says Bishop. 'Everybody was slightly shitting themselves. Will the FIA allow us to do this? Should we have a cocktail party at the Australian Grand Prix, or will it seem triumphalist? Should we be more humble?'

Bishop's role was clear. 'The job was to rebuild the reputation of the team in the eyes of the media, fans and sponsors,' he says. 'And we did do that. I am proud of being part of the team that did that.' It was no easy task but aided in no short order by the mercurial talent of a young Hamilton in only his second F1 season, a driver for whom Bishop has enormous respect.

'We went down to Australia and Lewis won. Grown men were weeping. They had thought they would all lose their jobs and we won. We beat Ferrari, the old enemy. It was an extraordinary feeling,' he remembers.

'Then Ferrari won a few races, then we went to Monaco and we won. I still can't talk about those moments without the hairs on the back of my neck standing up. We had this defensive pessimism and yet little Lewis kept winning. Then we got down to Interlagos and we all know what happened there. He won the championship on the last corner of the last lap of the last race, it was Roy of the Rovers stuff. Unbelievable. I love Lewis, I absolutely love, admire, respect and hold him in the highest esteem. One of the very best drivers we have ever seen, an utter privilege to work with and always lovely to me. He is a really good guy.'

Bishop it transpired was as good at managing communications as he had been at writing about them, but rebuilding McLaren's reputation, even given Hamilton's heroics, required every facet of the comms director's skill.

'It's all about storytelling,' he says. 'What would we like people to be saying about us? What more about us that they are not saying now? So you must come up with some objectives that are both strategic and commercial – the latter because they are why the sponsors will renew – that is a big piece of work.

'Then we look at the assets we have: drivers, senior people, the McLaren Technology Centre, the brand, the technology. How we can utilize those people and those things to help deliver the objectives. Then you have a comms strategy and we think of ways to story-tell that. This could be simple like holding a press conference, or hosting interviews but managing them to ensure that as part of the process the message is incorporated and in nurturing as many and as diverse a concert of outlets as possible.'

The access keeps the media on board as well as the team and its sponsors. It is another fine balancing act. A corporate lecture will not become news regardless of who delivers it, while heavy-handed threats generate only poor publicity and certainly no affection for teams but finagling a middle ground is where it pays off.

The popular perception that a comms director is solely engaged in a relentless battle to keep the media out of a team's business is not one to which Bishop subscribes. 'People think PR is all about control but it's not about control; we are in the entertainment business,' he says. 'I have always wished that when drivers come into *parc fermé*, the visor goes up and in goes the microphone for some raw, emotional quotes. It would have made my job harder but made for rich, authentic content.'

The drivers, of course, are at the heart of much of these activities and a consideration in any communications planning. But the director must also be able to react and think quickly and coherently to manage their charges, the best and most singular of which will always stray from their media training and even pre-prepared lines.

'I worked with Lewis who is a beautiful person and a wonderful driver but often difficult,' recalls Bishop. 'He wasn't pleased because the stewards at Monaco penalized him in 2011 and he famously said, "Maybe it's because I'm black. That's what Ali G says. I don't know."'

The chief steward that day was Lars Österlind, who was scandalized at being accused of overseeing a process that allegedly had penalized a driver for the colour of his skin. It was a huge problem for Hamilton and McLaren in the making.

'I said to Lewis, "You have to apologize." He said, "I ain't saying sorry,"' recounts Bishop. 'Sometimes you have to just think of the *mot juste*. I realized if Lewis did not say sorry it was going to be a real problem, a formal report, even a three-race ban for accusing the FIA stewards of racism. I remember saying to Lewis, 'It's now Sunday evening. We have to address this even if you don't say the word sorry. If you don't do that you will wake up tomorrow and you might not be an F1 driver, so give tomorrow morning's Lewis Hamilton the choice.

'If you get this wrong now and don't do it and snub them, as they have asked to see you, they might throw the book at you, and you might have a three-race ban. Give the Lewis of tomorrow, who won't be as furious as you are now, the chance. Keep your options open. In the end he did exactly that and said something along the lines of "it wasn't my intention to cause offence" and they thanked him for saying so. Crisis averted.'

Here then was the comms director *in excelsis* combining candour with willingness to speak truth to power and still walk away to a flight home with every party satisfied.

Fast thinking indeed, but in other cases, as with Vettel, there can be a far more structured plan in place with an entire strategy based around a driver's willing participation because it has touched a chord with them.

When the four-time champion Vettel joined Aston Martin, he knew the car would not be challenging for a championship. He had left Ferrari with disappointment on both sides without the title that he and the team so fervently desired, and by the time he joined Aston, the German was bored of the same old questions about Ferrari. He was at this point in his career an older, more mature driver and person with a family and was becoming far more interested in the world his children would inherit and what he could do from the F1 bubble to ensure his part in it was to make a positive contribution.

Bishop embraced his aims enthusiastically, a chance to push the envelope of what a driver could do and moreover what a driver could actually be.

'He wanted to do something more interesting and I never told him but internally we called it "The Saint Seb programme",' says Bishop. 'He does a lot of reading, and he would come to you and talk about some issue he was interested in. So to turn Seb into a saint was our strategic plan for what we wanted the fans, the sponsors, the media to think of us. Of course we never called it that publicly.

'We would brainstorm ideas for Saint Seb. He liked them, he realized he could do them and he did them well. He realized he was doing stuff that wasn't boring. He has a social conscience, he has three kids, he worries about the planet. He has liberal views and he thought, "It's wrong that Hungary should pass this law saying gay people should not be depicted positively in the media. I am going to say it's wrong." He saw the world agreed and the world applauded. That was Saint Seb.'

A host of projects followed. Vettel spoke out publicly on the environment, on LGBTQ+ rights, and the more he did the more he and his team felt empowered.

The campaign peaked for Bishop in a single day in London in 2022, in what must count as one of the masterpieces of comms direction, beyond a racetrack. Vettel began the day at the Feltham Young Offenders Institution, a prison for teenage boys, where they were launching a car mechanic unit, and Vettel met the inmates and made a speech. He followed it with a visit to a school in a deprived part of London before making history by becoming the first driver to appear on the BBC's political debate programme *Question Time*. On the show the panel of politicians are usually joined by one outlier, perhaps a celebrity, writer or musician, selected for their interest in current affairs. A tough ask for anyone not from the UK and whose first language is German.

Yet Vettel stepped up. 'I explained it to him, that it had been going for forty-two years, an institution on British TV, that it was quite tough and tricky and I asked if he would like to go on it,' recalls Bishop. Vettel agreed and Bishop extensively briefed him on the issues of the day knowing that among them Vettel's firm stance on action being required against the climate emergency and the environment would open him to accusations of being a hypocrite. It did but he handled it all with dignity and skill, even down to having to think on his feet in response to an unprepared-for question about whether Finland should join NATO.

Bishop was enormously happy at having pulled off a PR coup as Saint Seb reached an audience far beyond race fans and in so doing may well have changed some minds about the sport and encouraged others to give it a try. Almost all of Aston Martin's sponsors were delighted, too.

'Being in the garage in 2008 when Lewis won was an extraordinary moment, swept up in the euphoria,' Bishop says. 'But I was just there; it wasn't my achievement. Yes it is one of the greatest moments in my life and it was special, but I didn't land it. If you land something that you worked out and made happen that's different, and getting Seb on *Question Time* was a great moment that my little team and I landed.'

'I thought he played a blinder,' he adds. 'He was so different. He was the one I could do the most groundbreaking things with off-track and in so doing I realized I was doing groundbreaking stuff myself.'

Bishop can also be counted as having been groundbreaking in another very important regard. When he joined McLaren in 2008 he was the first openly gay man in the F1 paddock. He had been unashamed of his sexuality all his life and felt no reason to change for F1 and the sport is better for it.

'I was a rarity in F1 and people now I am friendly with, like Damon Hill and Martin Brundle, have both said, "Before I knew you I didn't really know any gay people at all and it's been a learning process for me." In the paddock I was at something of a disadvantage because I was a bit of a fish out of water, but it would have been much harder if I had been a mechanic.'

Not that it was plain sailing as he acknowledges one incident that remains shocking and is instructive of how much the sport and indeed society has changed since, not least because of men like Bishop.

'I remember when *Little Britain* came out and I felt I was the only gay in the F1 village,' he says. 'I did get some homophobia, most of which was said behind my back, but there was one driver whom I won't name who called me the "fat faggot" habitually and to my face.'

Bishop counts Alex Wurz and Kevin Magnussen as the drivers who became his two closest friends in F1, with his study proudly displaying helmets gifted by both men. His friendship with Wurz began when the Austrian, who is now chair of the Grand Prix Drivers' Association, made it clear he would not tolerate such abuse.

'I was walking down the paddock and I heard "faggot" and then "fat faggot" and I saw the driver who was saying it,' Bishop recalls. 'I walked on and he carried on repeating it. Alex Wurz saw this. He walked over to the driver and spoke to him loudly, saying, "You may think you are making Matt Bishop look like a cunt, but the only person you are making look like a cunt is yourself," and he walked away. I was so chuffed. Afterwards I went to Alex and thanked him. He said, "Don't worry," and that was the beginning of our friendship.'

F1 now has many openly LGBTQ+ personnel and a commitment to diversity and inclusion precipitated by Bishop and drivers he counts as allies such as Vettel, Hamilton and Wurz making their voices heard. Bishop has gone on to be a founder of the Racing Pride group which promotes LGBTQ+ inclusivity across all motorsport. He has also managed to add his name to his family's grand literary tradition by publishing his first non-motorsport book, *The Boy Made the Difference*, a novel fictionalizing the experiences of his generation of gay men to recount what it was like to live and often die against the backdrop of the HIV/AIDS crisis of the 1980s and 1990s.

The title is apt, for Bishop has always set out to make a difference, to make the role of communications director proactive, to be about driving a narrative rather than merely reacting to it and many drivers owe him a debt for doing so with such finesse.

'People sometimes expect a comms person to wave a magic wand to fix a problem or a mistake,' he says. 'If the team have done something stupid or negligent or bad, it will not be easy. So the comms person must get involved early on. A successful comms director knows it's not what you say about something, it's what you actually *do*.'

THE PIT MECHANICS

CHAPTER 12

THE PIT MECHANIC

FRAZER BURCHELL
NUMBER TWO MECHANIC - MCLAREN FORMULA 1 TEAM

'I am front jack on the pit-stops, the idiot who stands in front of the car. It's the job that carries the most risk; it's the ballsy job. It's up to the driver how late he stops when he comes into the box. If he comes in with all four wheels locked up and the steering wheel at ninety degrees, I know full well he is not going to stop. The best way to describe the front jack is, well, it's a bit like being punched in the face.'

Trust in what is a fundamentally dangerous situation, requiring perfect timing and an almost imperceptible sense of judgement, has become second nature for Frazer Burchell. Yet it is very much in the intensity of these moments in F1 that the McLaren mechanic is in his element. At his absolute best throwing himself into the hands-on business of racing, Burchell is at the very top of his game among the tool-wielding artistes of the F1 garage.

The number two mechanics are very much the sharp instruments of F1 teams. They are the shock troops, well trained, purposeful and adaptable, and they must deliver absolute perfection in the standard of their car build and maintenance week in, week out, over a punishingly long season, as well as being able to react quickly and with focused skill when required at the shortest notice, as Burchell attests.

'If a driver bins it, the first thing you are concerned about is, is he OK? The reaction then is very controlled but yes, it can be crazy,' he says. 'It can be pure chaos if you need to turn that car round in two hours. You will have two or three people working on top of you. I know and I trust the other mechanics which is as well since there is a good chance I am going to have someone's balls in my face and someone will be lying beneath me putting a low wishbone on while I am fitting a top wishbone.

'It is all about trust. You are all trying to work on top of each other as much as you can without getting in each other's way. From the outside it may look like a lot of screaming and shouting but it is actually a dance. It is an extremely well-rehearsed routine.'

Burchell is an unmistakeable figure on the grid, tall and slim with a shock of mousey brown hair, and usually sporting a broad grin. A man at ease with himself, then, but he can also cut an authoritative figure in proximity to Lando Norris's car that might be considered unusual in one so young. Despite being only thirty-one years old, it is a sense of calm assurance he has very much earned. Burchell has a calling. The carbon fibre, the steel, the intricacies of making it all work, of putting pieces together and taking them apart with absolute commitment has fascinated this young man almost his entire life, ever since he made the business of working on racing cars his singular intent as a teenager.

Indeed, back then so committed was he to his task that Burchell decided to follow a somewhat unorthodox route. 'When I was thirteen at school a lot of the bad pupils went off and did day release to college: courses like mechanics or bricklaying,' he explains. 'But I knew I wanted to get into motorsport, so I wanted to go and do mechanics on day release. The problem was my grades were good enough for them to say "no", but I insisted and still went ahead and did it. So I went to college for one day a week from when I was fourteen to when I was sixteen, doing the same course the naughtier kids were doing and did my exams as well. Even then I was absolutely set in wanting to work in motorsport.'

Burchell was born in Dorking and grew up in Surrey where he followed the wayward kids on day release. Dad was a firefighter and Mum a receptionist. His great-grandad Frederick G Brooking had raced an Aston Martin at Goodwood and specialized in Riley engines at his garage in Rusper in West Sussex, but it was his grandad Antony Brooking, who had been a mechanic, whose career he chose to follow.

The attraction, he explains, was very much in the practicality of the challenge. Burchell is intriguing and unusual in that it was this, much more so than the competitive racing aspect, that first stirred his interest in entering motorsport.

'I have always been very practical, always built stuff, always been very hands-on. I am very creative with my hands,' he says. 'I am not someone who could do an office job. I am the type of person who will build their own house, I have project cars and bikes; anything like that I will take apart and build.

'Wanting to strip stuff and build stuff, to be outside and in an environment that is constantly changing is what attracted me more to motorsport than the actual racing side of it.'

Indeed when forced to choose, for Burchell it transpires he could almost take or leave the sporting side of racing, as long as he was still allowed to wield a spanner in the garage.

'If I have a race weekend off I won't watch the race,' he admits with a smile, knowing how unusual an admission this is. 'But the bit I enjoy is the nitty-gritty side of it. How does it work? How does it go together? Because I want to put it together.'

Burchell is another of many of the participants in F1 for whom there have been very influential people or events that have helped shaped their lives. After taking his GCSEs he went on to study a BTEC national diploma in mechanical technology at East Surrey College. It was not a motorsport course but he once again found an outlet for his enthusiasm. A lecturer at the college, James Carpenter, had his own car which he would race and which he allowed the students to work on, once more on a day-release basis. Burchell put himself up to learn to build the car and go racing with him.

'My lecturer James was amazing,' he says. 'He had worked in the industry for years and he was very hands-on. He built everything himself, a full strip-down to nothing and a full build of the race car and he was meticulous. He was a good fabricator, a welder, engine builder – an engineer from the ground all the way up.'

This was a formative experience in more ways than one. It was not only a hands-on way of learning the trade, it was also essential for this very young man in coming to understand the level of the attention to detail that would be required in working on race cars. It demonstrated what the role really entailed, not only an ability to do the job but what was key was the high standard that was required each and every time.

'He was going to drive that car,' says Burchell, 'so for him it had to be done to a standard he was prepared to drive. I was working on it and I was the guy who would spanner it, so if he wasn't happy with my work he would not drive and wouldn't let me work on it. I learned from a very early age that all the detail, the work as well as the preparation, the cleanliness and tidiness you really need in motorsport, has to be there.'

For two years Burchell studied and went racing, committing himself to both with equal determination, insistent that despite his enthusiasm for the sport that he also kept his academic options open. Once more a considered and mature approach for a teenager. He achieved a triple grade distinction on his course, such that he could have gone on to university, which he considered. He could have taken a degree in motorsport engineering yet felt he had to make his mark by getting stuck in. 'For me my hands have always done the talking,' he says. 'A degree would have been proof of my intelligence, not proof of how practical I am.'

Instead, Burchell set about making it on his own terms. Even while at college he acted as a volunteer scrutineer at racing circuits hosting touring cars, GT Cup and British GT events because that was a sure-fire way to meet teams, with the entirely sensible rationale that even if he had no job with them yet, they would keep seeing his face. He handed out CVs in the paddock and told anyone willing to listen he would be ready to go to work when he finished his studies when he was eighteen. When that time came around he duly applied to as many teams as he could.

It paid off and he earned a job at DPR Motorsport in Guildford, who specialized in running Caterham sports cars. It was officially an apprenticeship which, with the experience he had already amassed, he did not need, but classified as such it meant the team would receive a small amount of government funding for doing it. That in turn required Burchell to attend college one day a week to take a theory course, a prospect that did not appeal to the young man who just wanted to go racing.

He offered instead to take all three of the theory tests in one day, did so, passed the lot and the college conceded that he did indeed not have to come in once a week. Point made, he went on to gain further invaluable experience running a Caterham full-time with the team, in charge of a car and soon clocking up wins with his driver.

Recognizing talent, Burchell was swiftly made a supervisor in charge of six cars, each with its own mechanic under his watch. A period that, for all that it was a low rung in the motorsport ladder, he remembers as crucial in both forging his character and abilities.

'These were skills that were key to the job,' he says. 'It doesn't matter if you are under an awning at Brands Hatch or if you are at an F1 race in a million-pound garage. At the end of the day my job is to repair a race car and get it back on track for a certain time. That's key regardless of the highest level of motorsport or the lowest.

'You learn it all at the lower level of motorsport because everything is on you. If anything goes wrong on that car, it is all on you. So I got a very good understanding of setting a car up, of engines, gearboxes. If it had a crash I would fix it. If it crashed in race one I would fix it for race two, and in Caterhams that was sometimes every weekend. In F1 for all that it is so much more complex, it is ultimately the same. If the car is in the wall you would be ready to fix it against the clock. It doesn't matter what car you are fixing, you are still working against the clock and *that* is the most important part of it – I learned that on Caterhams.'

His skill paying off, he moved up the ladder with his driver into GT racing in the Blancpain Endurance Series, the Spa 24 Hours and the VLN Nürburgring Endurance Series. Yet by the tender age of twenty-one, Burchell was already considering what was next. Interestingly, such had been his tenacious pursuit of just wanting to be building and running cars, he had not really considered the very idea of F1 until he thought, well, why not give it a shot?

McLaren ran an apprenticeship for a trainee build and test technician with a two-year contract which Burchell thought was worth a go. Characteristically he gave it his all and his experience in applying is demonstrative of the standards F1 requires just to get a foot in the door. Three interviews were the opener, including with the team manager and chief mechanic, during which Burchell admits he felt he was thoroughly grilled but fought his corner with honesty, putting his case for being a mechanic that had experience and who liked nothing better than long hours and getting stuck in.

Was it enough to persuade the gatekeepers of the very highest level of the sport though? Not quite yet, and a further interview ensued to see how he coped as a person, his very human reaction to teamwork in a practical assessment with a mechanic observing him execute a brake and throttle construction on the bench.

Given an engineering drawing, Burchell had to assemble the parts and then take them apart, which he did, all par for the course. 'Then he stood next to me and said, "Right, reassemble it,"' he recalls. 'I did it, and this time he spoke to me as I was doing it, about what tool I used at what times, when to torque stuff up. It was all very simple stuff to me but I think it was also to see how well I can keep a conversation going while I was doing the practical job at hand. It was about how I could manage, about working and interacting, which we have to be able to do.'

McLaren duly signed on the dotted line, and for two years Burchell cycled through various departments learning all the ropes and what was required in stepping up to the level of F1. It was intimidating to an extent, he concedes. Not in terms of doing the job but rather in encountering the sheer compass of what competing in F1 requires.

'When I first walked in it was more of the large scale, the scale of what F1 is going to be like that struck me,' he says. 'I just wanted to get into the garage, to get to what I know. I know race cars, I know where my toolbox is, where the car is and what I am doing in between. But in this huge infrastructure with a canteen, meeting rooms, multiple offices and 300 or 400 designers above me, that was the bit that was completely new. Yet I found it exciting, the idea of having that many people all pushing for the same goal – that was exciting.'

Two years later he had completed the trainee role and immediately pushed for a chance to join the race team, laughing as he recalls the 'itchy feet' he was getting being away from the track for so long. A permanent job in car build followed, preparing gearboxes ready for the race team to take to meetings and the spare chassis, ensuring it was ready to be used if needed.

He also travelled, too, working extensively in Japan with Honda, McLaren's engine supplier at the time. There he would build the car that Honda would use to run on the dyno. The 'dyno', a phrase bandied about a lot in F1, refers to the dynamometer. It is a mechanical construction that allows the power and torque of an engine to be accurately measured by running it in a clean, controlled environment. Effectively a test chamber where the engine runs as realistically as possible but on a static bed.

To this end they will build a full car with chassis engine, gearbox and radiators that would then put in miles on the dyno bed, where the engine runs and the wheels turn against vast rollers set into the rig. It goes nowhere but delivers vital data. Requiring much of the same maintenance as a real car, Burchell gained more valuable hands-on experience in working on it.

Finally, after a year and half, in 2018 Burchell's ambition was met as he was moved up to the race team and on to the car of no less a driver than the double world champion Fernando Alonso.

He was now part of a quite exclusive club. Each car has four number two mechanics. Two rear-enders, one chassis and one front-end, and each as the job title suggests has specific areas of responsibility. The rear-enders, Burchell's first role, would handle what are known as the two external 'corners' at the back of the car. This includes the parts that attach the wheels to the car, the top and bottom wishbones, driveshaft, the brake assembly on both sides and the dampers and roll bar assembly. During a session they would also adjust ride height, roll bar and torsion bar changes.

The chassis number two mechanic would look after the floor stays that come off the chassis, the fuel cell, radiators and hydraulic systems among a range of vital tasks, while the front-end has the cockpit to look after. This includes basically anything that moves at the front of the car: the pedals, steering, bellcranks, which are part of the damper and roll bar assembly, and the two external front corners. They are also responsible for the driver, for his position in the cockpit down to the level of padding in the seat to ensure he is comfortable and belting him in before the race begins.

Burchell has done the full monty. He spent two years on Alonso's car as rear-ender and then two years on the chassis and is now the front-ender for Lando Norris. He, like all the mechanics, also has a role in pit-stops on the front jack, a thrill ride like no other part of the competition he absolutely relishes, for all that it is a dangerous game.

'The best way to describe the front jack is it's a bit like being punched in the face,' he says. 'From the side everyone can see you being punched in the face, because you can see motion, but if you are in front of something and can only see it coming towards you, you've got no depth of perception of speed. The car could be driving at 40 kph or 60 kph, so whenever you see a front jack guy get hit, from the side it's obvious that the car wasn't stopping, but that's not so obvious when you are standing right in front of it.

'The car always stops as late as it can, so I always have to assume that it is going to stop and 95 per cent of the time it does. The one time it doesn't is what you see on TV,' he adds, laughing. 'Lando is very aggressive into the box but he always stops very well. He comes in quick but he stops. I don't mind that. I have learned that his aggression is always controlled.'

As the man who looks after the driver on the grid in his final moments before the off, a strong relationship of course develops. It's one Burchell feels he has with Norris, a driver perhaps more than most who has always made a point of building strong ties with his mechanics. 'I have always been with Lando, and I have known him since he was a junior driver at McLaren,' says Burchell. 'Lando was nineteen when he first signed as a reserve, so he would come to race weekends as an unknown and would come out for dinner with us when we went out in the evenings.

'I see Lando out of work as well, though. We play golf together; we always have done as he loves his golf. We have always had a good relationship at work and outside of work, you have to. Lando is unique as quite often if his flight is the same night as us, he will come into the garage and help strip the car. He will chat with us and chill out; he won't sit in his driver's room or go back to the hotel, he will happily come into the garage and be with us instead. So we all see him as a friend as well as a driver.'

Of course the closer the relationship mechanics have with drivers only intensifies the emotions, the pleasure and the pain that are an inescapable part of competition. In 2021 at the Russian Grand Prix, Norris had taken his maiden F1 pole and with a consummate drive was leading and set for his first win until he stayed out too long on slick tyres when late rain hit the track. With just three laps to go he spun off and was forced to pit, his hard work and chances of a win laid to waste in a matter of moments. Drivers' feelings in such circumstances are widely publicized – a visibly upset Norris pronounced he was devastated at what had happened – but in the garage the pain is no less intense.

'It can hit hard. Let no one assume that what happens over a race weekend is not felt deep in the hearts and souls of those behind the scenes,' says Burchell. 'We qualified on pole – I had never qualified on pole in F1 before. There was such a buzz and energy on wheeling the car to the front of the grid, then being at the front of the grid for the national anthem. To lead the race throughout, and to then lose, that was soul-destroying.'

Yet what is genuinely telling about these often stoic stalwarts of F1 is the reaction afterwards. 'Everyone in the team had had a great weekend even though it was the highest high to the lowest low,' Burchell explains. 'But what mattered was how the whole garage then responded to doing their normal job. Getting the car, stripping the car and going home. You might have six hours of frustration but you still have a job to do. It can feel like a massive kick in the balls but everyone gets over it because we know we have a job to do.'

This then is perhaps at the heart of the passion felt by every mechanic in F1. There is no sense this is simply a job but rather a vocation. Burchell knew this was what he wanted to do since he was a teenager and it has not disappointed. He wanted to be hands-on and feel the buzz of being part of a practical process and could not have been more successful in that endeavour. After a long journey, and with surely more to come, the things that matter most in F1 remain part of a simple creed Burchell has adopted from the very beginning and which has served him well since he chose day release with the naughty boys over the classroom.

'Pride in your work is everything,' he says. 'Making sure it is done in a certain way and a certain order and the right way of doing the job, I learned that very early on. It is all the more important with the stakes so high in F1. It's the small things that have to be correctly done, meticulously done and that's where we mechanics are, right on top of that.'

CHAPTER 13

THE CFO

RUSSELL BRAITHWAITE
CHIEF FINANCIAL OFFICER - MERCEDES-AMG PETRONAS F1 TEAM

'Since F1 introduced the budget cap in 2021, the technical regulations and the sporting regs and financial regs, well, I would go as far as to say that they almost have equal weighting now in the way they are discussed and organized in the team. Now, everyone is very aware of the financial regs and their impact on going racing and you can tell. When I started with Mercedes F1 the financial team was sixteen people, but today there are over forty of us.'

As Russell Braithwaite acknowledges, there was a time when running the business side of an F1 team was considered a cursory task. The successful management of finance was an addendum to the relentless pursuit of performance. Post cost cap, the role has become vital, the channelling, organization, monitoring and control of a finite amount of funding now such an integral part of the sport it is a fundamental differentiator for success when going racing on a Sunday.

Braithwaite has been nothing if not relentless in the pursuit of his chosen career since he decided that he wanted to be an accountant at the age of thirteen. However, he is aware this might appear somewhat less appealing an ambition than that of his colleagues at the sharp end of taking cars racing. 'Although I am an accountant I'm not as boring as it sounds,' he says with a broad grin and no little veracity.

The forty-eight-year-old is fine company, witty and honest, and he is unafraid to display some self-deprecating humour. At the same time he is a clearly intelligent man, one who has demonstrated no little commitment and skill to rise to what is now one of the most senior positions in any F1 team. Having joined the Mercedes F1 team in 2018, his insights into how the financial nature of the sport has changed in that time are fascinating. Since then, there have been two periods to the role of an F1 CFO: the pre- and post-cost cap eras.

Braithwaite had already been a CFO with Mercedes road cars for seven years when he took the job with the team. He was highly qualified and experienced, with a strong grasp of the automotive business, but F1 was a whole other ball game.

'If I had arrived with the same attitude that I carried through my career to that point, I don't think the F1 team would have let me come back for a second week.' He explains. 'The scales were very different, the measurements were very different and the speed at which things were operating were all completely different. Things you would just say no to in ordinary business cases were a definite yes, because there was lap time in it.

'I had to realize very quickly that the top currency is lap time and performance and to find a way to balance that with the other objectives of financial control. Everything was tenths of seconds or milliseconds, not denominations you used in any other financial area.'

This was no little change for Braithwaite, who was adapting in short order. Pre cost cap, when a team like Mercedes existed largely as a marketing branch of the brand, the financial largesse to achieve success was taken as something of a given. The money merely another weapon in the team's arsenal. Something else the CFO had to come to terms with.

'I went to a meeting in my first week, a capital review board,' says Braithwaite. 'Someone wanted a tool that would change the precision measurement by some very, very fractional denominations and it was going to cost a lot of money. Silently I thought: "I'm not sure that makes sense," but I watched the room and everyone was absolutely bang on that we needed to have it. I realized I had to recalibrate and be able to make decisions that you might have said no to in the past. I needed a similar recalibration when drivers' salaries came up too ...'

This was, he swiftly understood, as with almost every role in F1, an enormously collaborative process. Braithwaite knew he had to strike up a close relationship with engineers, to understand and sympathize with the very singular mindset with which they operated; the pursuit of performance with an intensity and relentlessness to which everything else was subjugated.

'I learned that until the graph has a zero return in performance it makes sense for an engineer to keep chasing that. The currency for that to some extent prior to the cost cap wasn't important, as long as it was returning performance towards the key objective, to win.'

He sums this up succinctly in describing how everything was channelled to this one end and how his part in it was to facilitate that by one means or another. Effectively at that time there were only two answers to spending and both of them ultimately amounted to 'yes'.

'No was not really the answer we would give in the uncapped environment because the brand is what we are trying to enhance so we wanted to win,' he says. 'So we would just consider: have we got the resources yes, or have we got the resources no, and if no, well how can we find the resources?'

This more free-spending approach underwent a fundamental change with the budget cap. The intent was twofold. Firstly, to end the differentiation in spending between the big three teams – Ferrari, Red Bull and Mercedes – who had enormous budgets and the rest of the field who simply could not match these numbers. By putting a ceiling on spending the aim was to bring about a gradual levelling of the playing field.

The secondary purpose was to end the spending arms race that had escalated among the leading teams and to ensure that every team could be financially sustainable such that they would finally start to turn a profit. A target which, remarkably despite the great swathes of money washing round in the sport, was rarely if ever achieved.

It was, outside of amendments to the technical regulations, one of the most significant changes the sport had undergone in decades and required a major transformation in attitudes and practices.

At which point Braithwaite found himself at the sharp end of managing a fundamental shift in how Mercedes had to operate, in genuinely holding the purse strings. Yet, contrary to expectations, rather than being a positively Herculean task, he believes the shift has in its own way made his job more straightforward.

'Now it's easier, which is the opposite of what you might expect,' he explains. 'As an example, someone in a very important role came to me in my induction week and said: "I am so-and-so and this is my role in the team but we won't meet much, you just need to make sure you keep giving me the money." I thought, "OK." I was very new at that time. That person is now in my office two or three times a week since the cap. It's very interesting to see how we have become integral and pivotal to performance in a way we weren't before.'

It stands to reason that this increased involvement might take the form of saying 'No', where previously the answer had always been 'Yes'. It has instead fostered a closer relationship between the financial and engineering wings of the team, a collective acknowledgement that now neither can act independently of the other.

'We have to come to the point collectively where we don't do certain things; we have to find that path together and that's really important,' says Braithwaite. 'We can do the cost cap in thirty minutes and we can be compliant. But the car might be the last one on the grid. The guys can make the car fastest but probably blow the cap, so unless we do it together we are in trouble.

'Of course we do say no to things but they are more to do with interpretation of regulations; we generally find an alignment in where the priorities for spending are. We don't have much conflict there because we find the right solutions together.'

This has necessitated a different method of working and one where the man who has pursued making the numbers work since he was a child found he was in his element. With it came the realization that such was the scale of the task it could only be met by an expansion of personnel on the financial side of the business.

'We had an organization that could not be compliant unless we changed,' he says. 'That became a very intense discussion with the team and the engineers about what is the path, how we do it, how we interpret the regulations. We looked at the business and decided how we can spend more efficiently, how we can get more value in performance from each dollar.

'In that process I had a realization that this is my language. It was administrative in nature but it's now a performance differentiator, so I then had to work on interpreting and optimizing, on keeping control of people, costs and inventory in a way we have not had to do before.'

Every team is adapting to this new reality in different ways, but those that had the least or no cutting to do to meet the cap have had minimal levels of adaptation. At teams such as Mercedes, Braithwaite and his colleagues have found themselves hosting new forms of the decision-making process.

'In capital expenditure, we have a board that supports those purchases and now it's a bit like *Dragons' Den*,' he explains. 'We have an amount of budget to spend on capital investment and people come and say they want to do a project, and can they have the funding. They almost come and pitch to a little board. The first decision-makers are IT, technical engineering guys, operations and me to decide whether this is a good use of our limited resources. If it is, then we have to find the cash for it.'

Braithwaite's role, then, in either era, is one of control. To oversee and steer the financial governance of the team. This includes ensuring there is enough funding to run the organization, from being able to pay the drivers, to every other employee and all the suppliers. It also means managing income, to collect revenue from sponsors and from the F1 prize fund distributed amongst the teams at the end of the season, on a sliding scale according to their position in the Constructors' Championship.

Which might all sound a little dry, but for Braithwaite it is very much a labour of love. He always wanted to work in finance but the dream was to be managing it on an international stage and in the automotive sector. Mercedes F1 it transpires was pretty much the perfect destination and he is proud at having made it, while Mercedes could not have a CFO more suited to the task.

In his office at the team's factory in Brackley he stands up and darts over to a display stand across the room, returning with a model of a Mercedes CL500, a gift from a former boss during his time with Mercedes road cars. 'He gave it to me because it was the first car I ordered when I joined Mercedes,' explains Braithwaite. 'It was the best car they had at the time. It was top of the range and it was far too big and over the top for what I needed as a single guy, but it gives you an idea how addicted I was to them.'

This addiction had been long in gestation. Braithwaite had been obsessed since he was a child, when he admits he was 'fanatical' about cars. His first was an Audi 80 Sport his father had bought and surrendered to his pestering son, then he also acquired a Peugeot 205 GTi, before moving on to BMW 3 Series coupés.

At the height of his collecting he owned around twelve different cars, simply because of the sheer enjoyment they brought. A hoard he has since forgone but with one concession to the past in the form of a hobby that doubles up as a penance. 'I have a Peugeot 205 I am restoring at the moment,' he says. 'That 205 I had at a very young age, well I wrote it off. I am trying to correct that piece of history by restoring one.'

The interest in cars then was undeniable but there was no path that necessarily would take him to F1 and indeed, it was not a straightforward affair. He was born and raised in Northampton where his father was a mechanical engineer and his mother a housewife and clerk at Barclaycard. He grew up watching F1 and went to the British Grand Prix for the first time in 1991 as a teenager, an experience he describes as the hook that pulled him into the sport.

For one so young he was, however, already singularly focused. 'I was very clear all along I wanted to be an accountant, by thirteen years old,' he says. 'I knew that was my path, what I wanted to achieve, so it was very easy and I went on and did an accounting and finance degree.'

F1 was still not on the radar, but Braithwaite did know he wanted an automotive element to his career, alongside the chance to work internationally.

With a 2:1 from the University of Leicester completed,

Braithwaite then qualified to become an accountant with the Association of Chartered Certified Accountants. He went on to work for several companies including Granada TV before an opportunity with DaimlerChrysler opened up in 2004 running the finances of the Mercedes-Benz after-sales business in the UK. After several years he wanted to step up to a CFO post and in 2011 was given the chance to do so for Mercedes in Dubai, heading up the company's sales operations across the Middle East.

After Mercedes' purchase of Brawn GP in 2010 and an increasing number of races in the Middle East, Braithwaite developed a relationship with the team and the principal Toto Wolff, who decided to bring him on board in 2018. It was an opportunity he relished but one that brought new demands and pressure.

'I was very happy but quite apprehensive because it is super high profile in the group,' he says. 'I could bring value but I was not well connected with the headquarters nor did I know inside F1 well; I only knew it as a fan. But I was convinced I could make the adaptation that was required so I threw myself into it.'

With Mercedes on a roll, having taken four consecutive drivers' and constructors' titles at that point, Braithwaite's biggest concern was that he would not upset this roaring juggernaut. 'It sounds strange but I was desperate at the start not to be the reason this success stopped,' he says. 'I felt I had joined a team that had proven itself to be so successful so I wanted to slot in and make sure I could perform. That was my first objective, privately.'

An objective he fulsomely achieved as the Mercedes machine managed its eighth consecutive constructors' title in 2021. The playing field has changed through that period and since, so he has of course had to adapt around his central charge of controlling the finance of the business.

Now Braithwaite starts with a plan with the ultimate target of extracting maximum performance from the car within the budget cap. In the case of Mercedes suffering with a car down on pace in both the 2022 and 2023 seasons, that plan inevitably has to be adaptable as the season progresses, making the CFO role very much a dynamic one.

He must not only adjust for demands from engineers as they attempt to come to grips with the car, but also allow for inflation adjustments or changes in rule interpretations and clarifications that mean something is allowed that was previously banned. He is managing a finely balanced equation. The purpose is to come as close to the cap as possible but with no risk of going over it and suffering a penalty, while avoiding being too far beneath the limit and losing potential performance.

To this end there is a defined methodology to the process that has required the substantial expansion of financial staff. They employ systems to monitor and control the business, including now a second level of observation, which Braithwaite refers to as bilingual reporting, so that there is a comprehensive knowledge and management of where the money is going. It is an extensive structure which strikingly, while not quite real time, keeps the numbers up to date mere hours after every race weekend.

Braithwaite describes what he calls the three pillars of the financial organization at Mercedes. They are the commercial team, the performance team and the group in charge of tax and accounting. Each produces monthly reports which are given to the shareholders. However, for the task of meeting the cost cap, the agenda is far more frequent. The three pillars meet in a forum every week, to consider the sporting landscape politically and whether the planned financial achievements are on target or not, all of which feeds back into management meetings to assess reaction to said results.

The team must also consider potential damage and repair and replacement costs and plans for such with a damage budget. If there is a big accident, once Braithwaite knows the driver is OK his next immediate consideration is the impact on spending as it could be a genuine issue for potential performance since a run of bad luck and prangs could ultimately cost the team as much as a major upgrade.

Alongside which, Braithwaite must also pursue a level of proactive behaviour on the team's behalf, including lobbying the FIA for action when the high rate of inflation in 2022 and 2023 drastically hit all of the F1 teams' financial planning.

There are then a myriad range of different demands requiring attention from Braithwaite and his team. To keep a handle on all this, they host a series of different consultations between engineers and finance and between finance and the key stakeholders for the bigger picture issues. It is an almost ceaseless but essential exchange of information without which the immense complexity of the financial process would be unmanageable.

That it is taken enormously seriously in F1 is clear. 'A budget cap breach would be terrible from a performance and brand perspective,' confirms Braithwaite just as, to illustrate his point with perfect timing, the Mercedes technical director James

Allison enters his office looking for a word. 'That is always happening,' he says. 'It can just pop up like James coming in – that would be something to do with financial regulations I am sure.'

In 2021, Braithwaite was invited on to the podium in Bahrain to collect the constructors' trophy alongside Lewis Hamilton. As a black man he admires Hamilton's commitment to diversity within the sport and shares the driver's appreciation of its importance within F1.

'Race certainly hasn't prevented me [from succeeding] in any way but I have been aware of it,' he says. 'It is most interesting that post George Floyd and Black Lives Matter it has been become so much more of an issue. There has been a higher level of awareness and relevance. I work off a principle of meritocracy – if you are good enough and work hard and perform you will be rewarded.

'It's most important for me that meritocracy stays at the forefront. We don't want a quota system, we just want the best talent to have the opportunity so the right people can come to the fore. Lewis is the perfect example of that. He is good enough and he got through. It's really about equal opportunities.'

Braithwaite has certainly left nothing to chance. He has seized every opportunity he has had to make the numbers work in a role that has combined all the ambitions he held when growing up – and he is unashamedly pleased to be doing so.

'I love it. I love being part of the team,' he says. 'What I really enjoy about being at Mercedes is that for me this is not necessarily the pinnacle of my industry. You can be an accountant anywhere, it's a portable role, but a lot of the people I am working with here are at the very pinnacle of their industry. They are great minds, great talents and very bright people. It is super to be a part of that.'

CHAPTER 14

THE LOGISTICS COORDINATOR

SARAH LACY-SMITH
TRACKSIDE LOGISTICS COORDINATOR - MCLAREN FORMULA 1 TEAM

'When I started I was the first girl in the mechanics band at McLaren so there was a sense of can you do it? Can you really do it? I did have to prove myself, prove that I didn't mind getting carbon dust all over me and oil down my shirt. I had to prove I was not the typical girly girl, which at the track I am not and now, well, I'm one of their own.'

For Sarah Lacy-Smith it was always quite clear that if she made it to F1, a matter of oil or dust was never going to deter her pursuing what had been a quite singular ambition. From a childhood preferring Scalextric and Meccano to Barbie dolls, she showed a relentless determination to make it into racing, joining McLaren in 2014 and then going on to secure and master a little known but absolutely vital and complex role in managing the thousands of parts required to ensure any F1 car can take to the track.

A modern F1 car consists of approximately 14,500 components, each a bespoke element of what is a brand new prototype built from scratch every year. At every circuit, each item required for a race weekend must be managed with a level of redundancy included in the planning. Replacements must be factored in to allow for wear and tear, damage and failure. They must be organized meticulously, tracked and monitored and at hand for use at a moment's notice.

When a driver puts a car into a wall and pieces of it fragment and cartwheel across the track, that it can then be rebuilt, often at a seemingly impossible pace, to make it to the next session, is in no little part down to logistics coordinators such as Lacy-Smith.

'It's not a great feeling when you see a car crash, but you have to get on with it,' she says. 'As soon as we know the driver is safe, my first thought is: "What do I need to replace to start kitting it up?" If I see a big crash, even before you have seen the car when it has come back in, we will be out the back kitting up what we think they will need to replace, so they can get it fitted as quickly as possible.

'We look at what happened. For example, have they gone in

Right: Marianne Hinson: 'When I started I was very clearly in a massive minority; I was the only girl in the aero department when I began at Jordan. But nobody has ever discouraged me or made me think I couldn't do it. I never felt that. I never felt discouraged or unwelcome.'

Left: Neil Ambrose: 'When I first arrived at Red Bull I felt it was a big deal. You could approach people like Christian Horner or Adrian Newey. People you watch on television and now I am talking to and working at the same place as them. That was enough to make my head explode.'

PERONI
ASTON MARTIN
Cognizant
aramco
JCB
ASTON MARTIN
Cognizant

ROLEX
vuse
McLaren
vuse
DEWALT
Haas

Above: Russell Braithwaite (left): 'I had to very quickly realize that the top currencies are lap time and performance, and to balance those with the other objectives of financial control. Everything was tenths of seconds or milliseconds, not denominations you use in any other financial area.'

Top left: Matt Bishop (right) with Sebastian Vettel: 'Seb wanted to do something more interesting and I never told him but internally we called it "The Saint Seb Programme". To turn Seb into a saint was our strategic plan for what we wanted the fans, the sponsors, the media to think of us.'

Bottom left: Frazer Burchell (right): 'It is all about trust. You are all trying to work on top of each other as much as you can without getting in each other's way. From the outside it may look like a lot of screaming and shouting but it is actually a dance. It is an extremely well-rehearsed routine.'

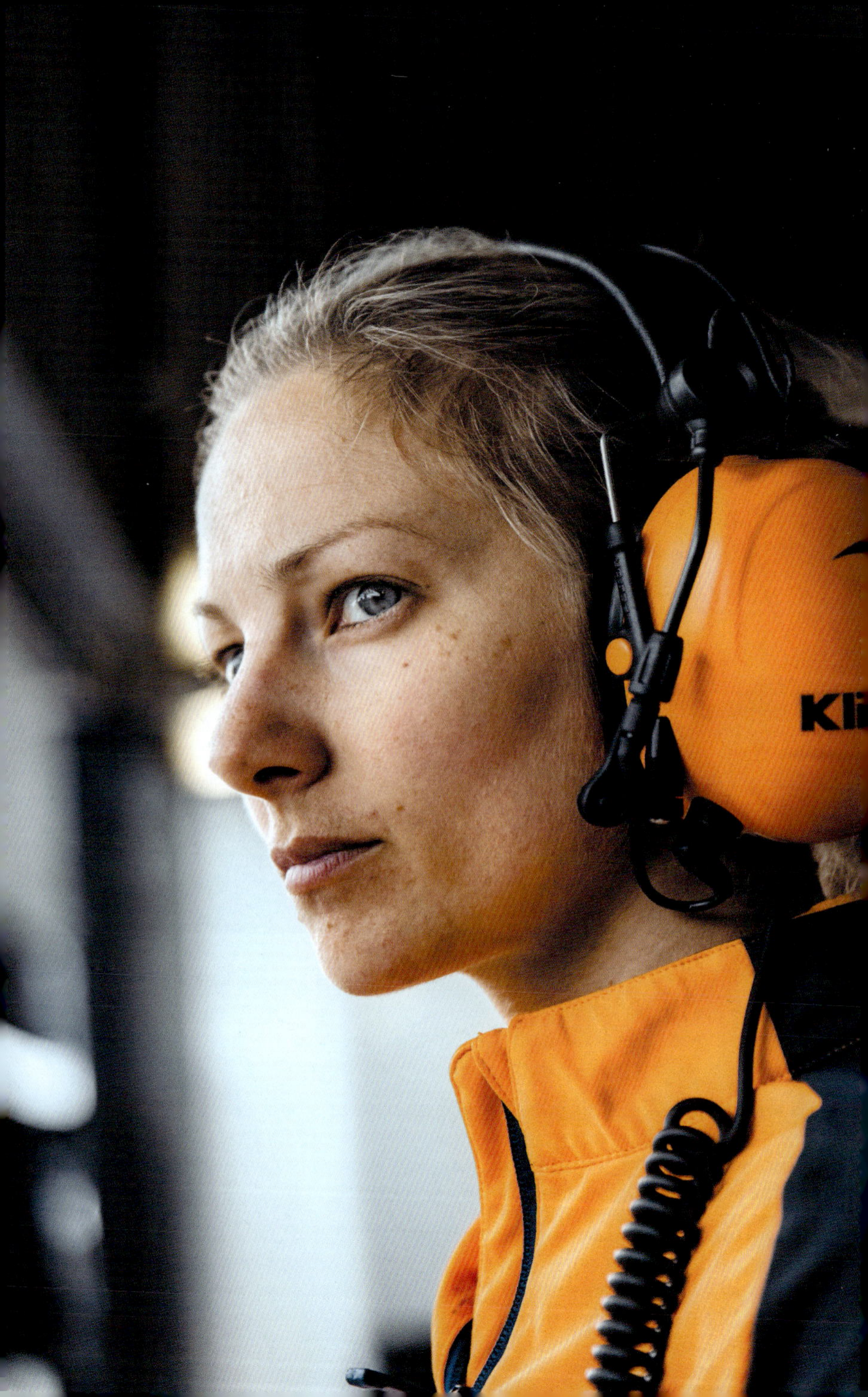

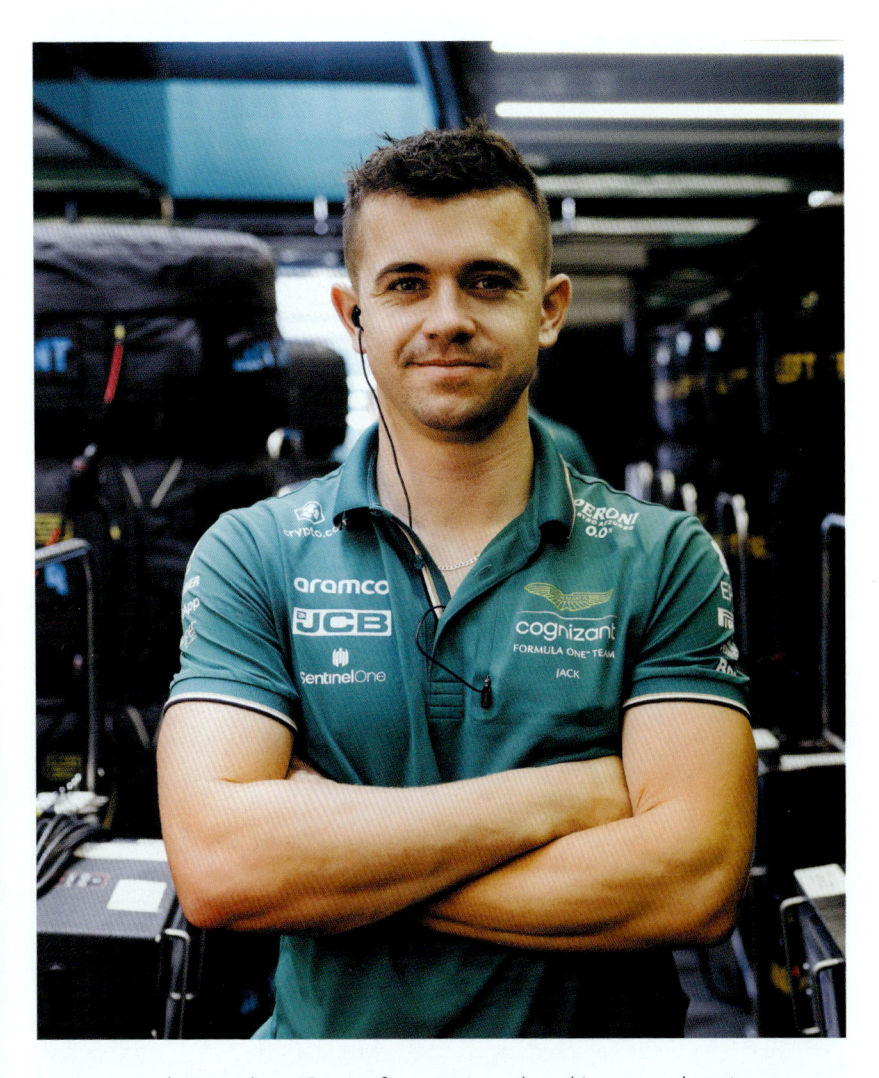

Above: Jack Partridge: 'On my first race weekend I was on the pit crew, and it was exciting, nerve-wracking, all the emotions rolled into one. We do so much practice but five years on it is still such an exciting part of the job.'

Left: Sarah Lacy-Smith: 'As a child I was never given the Barbies or the dolls. Mum didn't give me the girly stuff. If I'd wanted a doll I could have had one, but I found my brother's Meccano and Scalextric far more intriguing.'

Above: Guillaume Rocquelin: 'The step between motor racing in general and F1 is massive and it is getting bigger every day. The F1 car is so much lighter, so much quicker; everything is designed with no compromise whatsoever, a different beast, a big eye-opener.'

Below: Kari Lammenranta: 'Some of it I felt came naturally and some of it didn't but you start getting it – why things are done in a certain way. You wonder why we are going into it in such detail, but after a while you understand because that is what you have to do with a racing car.'

Above: Victoria Johnson with Nico Rosberg (left) and Lewis Hamilton (right): 'Lewis held my hand, put his arm round my shoulder and took me out there and put me on the step I was meant to stand on. That's Lewis, he made it perfect.'

Below: Lucas Blakeley: 'I was a super-passionate kid about racing and wanting to be an F1 driver. I used to put all my karting kit and my helmet on just to drive round Monaco in my bedroom on the F1 game.'

from the front? So it could be bits on the floor at the front are missing, so let's get a new keel panel out, suspension legs at the front, any elements you consider will have taken damage.'

When she references 'out the back', Lacy-Smith is describing her domain in the paddock. At the back of the garage or just behind it are the precious racks over which she presides. She and colleague Callum Turner maintain the collections of parts that ensure the team can entirely rebuild a car if required, but where they also facilitate its optimal running and maintenance. They can upgrade and replace parts that have reached the limit of their safe or reliability lifetime, or swap in those of a differing specification according to set-up requirements. This includes everything that is on the chassis, all the monocoque parts, the fuel system, the brake ducts, the suspension, the hard lines, the hoses, all the items teams refer to as 'the internals'.

A new brake duct, for example, would require not only all the parts for the duct itself but also those to build it on to the car, necessitating a striking, elephantine ability for recall.

'You have to be quite good at memorizing stuff,' Lacy-Smith notes with wry amusement. 'Because you often don't have time to go and find the list of parts, so you kind of just have to know it.'

Delivered by air freight for flyaway races and by truck in Europe, she has five racks at each race; large, portable storage units housing thousands of items, enough for three full car sets of components. Three of the racks consist of drawers housing the smaller parts, across two with twenty drawers and one with eight.

They are home to what she calls 'the nitty gritty bits'. From the bolts to the suspension legs, from harnesses and hoses, to all the parts for electronics. Two other racks are shelved to host the larger items such as the heat shields, tail pipes, turbine pipes and smaller body work panels such as the bonnets.

It might then be considered the garden shed screw storage tidy on an infinitely grander and more complex scale, with Lacy-Smith as its curator. They might not be as noticeable as the front of house race strategists or team principals, but she and her colleagues are invaluable to their work.

'We are based in the garage, so we work with information that can come from a mechanic or an engineer,' she explains. 'If it is a change in spec, then that would come from an engineer saying, "We need to change the brake system; can you please get this set-up ready?" Usually different components make up a different set-up. Everyone has a brake set-up sheet so we know how to kit out different configurations. While if it is a broken part that will come from a mechanic who will tell us what we need to replace.'

There is a major element of management and teamwork to this role that requires great care and diligence to avoid errors or shortfalls. 'The parts are built at McLaren or purchased and it's a mix of us and the factory coordinators that make sure all the items are in the racks,' she adds. 'It's our job to feed back if we have used something or something is broken. We feed that back to the factory team who then replace those parts and send them back out to us. We have to track the stock as well, so every single part has a part number or a serial number and it is stocked to a drawer or to a location. It's a constant challenge and constantly changing; every race has something different to throw at you and it's fun as well.'

That the thirty-two-year-old still derives great pleasure from her work seems justifiably deserved after she always prioritized her ambitions to pursue a career in something that genuinely appealed to her.

Lacy-Smith speaks of her road to F1 with a voice inflected with humour and an endearing self-deprecating honesty. 'As a child I was never given the Barbies or the dolls. Mum didn't give me the girly stuff,' she says. 'If I'd wanted a doll I could have had one, but I found my brother's Meccano and Scalextric far more intriguing. I would get Barbies every now and then from birthday parties, but I would just cut their hair off. That was far more interesting to me than playing with them.'

It was a fondness for racing and engineering pastimes that reflected a kid who was perhaps unusually already considering the future in an entirely pragmatic fashion. 'I suppose I was an odd child,' she says. 'I was always thinking about what I wanted to do when I grew up and it was never an astronaut or something like that; I was very practical about what I wanted to do.

'My mum always brought me up to think about what to do with your life, what to get into and how to get there. She was very encouraging, and I think she would have loved to do something like what I eventually did.'

Lacy-Smith was brought up in the village of Sherfield on Loddon, near Basingstoke, in a family who enjoyed watching F1 but had no motor racing background or connections. She and her brother took to watching F1 themselves and in 2000, simply based on her brother's fondness for the colour green, followed Minardi because of the bright livery on their M02 car.

'We were quite young, nine or ten, but anything green for my brother was the prime thing, so we supported Minardi for years just because they were green,' she recalls. 'I didn't specifically like one driver. I was always more interested in the racing than the drivers and that's almost the same now; I am still more interested in the cars than the drivers.'

Minardi's colour scheme might have been as far as her interest went but for happenstance putting ideas in her head. 'When I was about ten or eleven, I was getting under my dad's feet, so he sent me to this posh car showroom round the corner to get me out of the way,' she says. 'I saw a TVR in the greeny-purple and I thought, "I like that. I want to do something like *that*." It was a beautiful car; there was something about it. That was my first notion of what I wanted to do; that it was in the automotive field.'

She admits that at this stage F1 seemed an awfully long way off and was, unsurprisingly given her character, realistic about how hard it would be, but knowing she just wanted to work within automotive design set her sights on giving it a shot at the very least. As a female in what remains a male-dominated industry, it was inevitably a journey of some travail and complication. Not least in having pursued the requisite GCSEs and A levels only to find some mindsets were still not ready.

'There were a lot of barriers and a lot of people doubting,' she recalls. 'In my school I spoke to the careers lady and I said: "I think I want to design cars." I mentioned that I was not sure if I wanted to go into the styling and the aerodynamics or the engines. For some reason she picked up on "styling" and wrote down "interior design".

'About a year later she rang my mum and asked how I was getting on and if I had pursued my interior design degree. My mum absolutely tipped at her and said: "No, she's going to university to do an engineering degree." Mum really didn't like it.'

Having established that it was carbon fibre, not scatter cushions, that held her attention, a four-year degree with a Master's followed at Loughborough – itself still apparently somewhat unsure as to her intent. 'In 2008 even at university, at my interview the bloke right at the end said, "You do know this is about designing the engines?" And I said, "Yes, is that all right?" There were a lot of little comments like that; you pick up on them.'

Fortunately, she had the encouragement from family to brush such slights aside. 'There were quite a few points like that where if I hadn't had my parents backing me it would have been quite hard,' she says. 'Mum and Dad backed me 100 per cent. They were always very supportive. They let me know I can just get on with it, that if I wanted to do something, I should do it.'

At university she came to realize that design was not the field she enjoyed most, but rather that project management was more to her liking, team leading to solve tasks being something she revelled in. Upon graduation, at twenty-three years old, Lacy-Smith applied for an operations role on the graduate scheme at McLaren on a two-year contract, the role designed to cycle new employees through a range of departments including purchasing, project planning and logistics.

For a young woman straight out of college, suddenly finding herself at the heart of one of F1's most successful and historic teams in a sport she had only dreamed of reaching was an enormous moment. 'It was quite surreal actually getting that job, the one you have been looking forward to but didn't think you would ever get,' she says. 'On day one it was pretty terrifying, but exciting. I am an anxious person so I was looking around going, "Oh my God, I am here!" It was months before I really felt that yes, this is what I do now.'

It was McLaren's good fortune they had found her too. She did not complete her two-year graduate scheme but was instead hired as a full-time member of staff within a year. Having obviously already impressed, she was given a full-time job in purchasing, liaising with suppliers on parts, orders and deadlines, but six months later she went for a role she preferred in logistics and was successfully made a factory parts coordinator in 2016.

This entailed ensuring that all the parts needed for her area of the car, the brakes and suspension, made it to the track. It meant working closely with the project management team, meeting deadlines and kitting up parts to get them out and ensuring the right quantities were in place. She was responsible in part then for filling the racks for the trackside team, a role she swiftly coveted.

'I realized at that point that the logistics team had people that went trackside,' she says. 'Then I knew I wanted to do that, but I had never even considered it before, largely because on TV you don't see all the supporting roles that exist in the paddock.'

After another seven months she had the place as trackside coordinator, attending every meeting and very much in what felt like her element, enjoying a role she swiftly learned was enormously intricate over a race weekend.

Having arrived on the Tuesday of the meeting, on the Wednesday, the car build day, everyone has to be ready to go. They go through what needs replacing from previous events and what needs servicing, a process which, as with everything in F1, is measured with acute attention to detail.

'We know what mileage components have done and at the previous race I will have done a report that tells the mechanics what they need to take off the car because it needs servicing or is out of life,' she explains. 'All the high-ticket items, the bits that would stop the car running if they broke, they all have a life number assigned to that part and measured in kilometres.'

This is an absolutely vital piece of administrative care that of course is not captured by the TV cameras, but that can result in an all too public display should it cause a failure.

'So a suspension leg, for example, will do four races,' Lacy-Smith explains. 'Then it needs to go back to the factory to be crack-checked, proofed, have the harness checked, the hose checked. There are other parts that after every single race they go back, or we use an NDT [non-destructive testing] technician trackside who can crack-check parts. They use an eddy current device to check parts with. A little machine that goes over metallic and carbon components and then they can see on the screen where they can tell if there are any cracks within the component.'

All of which it appears would be a logistical challenge of enormous complexity, but one aided by a special computerized virtual car that catalogues this 'lifeing' system. Every part is allocated a 'life code' designated by the design office when it is designed, which is logged on to the system. The virtual build then records every session the real thing does and any changes made to components within those sessions. It allows Lacy-Smith and Turner to monitor everything and at the end have a report on what needs changing subject to whether there is another race immediately to follow or indeed a further double-header.

They can then liaise with the factory to ensure a smooth flow of new parts and returns, keeping the entire repository stocked and running as the vast racing behemoth consumes all the parts required across a lengthy season.

As with many trackside personnel, Lacy-Smith must also turn her hand to not a little multitasking when not needed to manage the parts. She has been pit board operator for Fernando Alonso and Lando Norris and also during sessions been in charge of the fans deployed into the car on the radiator ducts and taking the front jack from the number one mechanic after it is pulled out from the car.

Alongside all of which there is often also even more prosaic work to be done, as her and Turner are required for unpacking duties as the weekend progresses and not just for the parts over which they hold dominion, but anything that rocks up at all.

'We are also responsible for unpacking all the deliveries that arrive, freight or vans,' she says. 'Loads of stuff comes, new parts, replacement parts. We once unpacked dumbbells in Budapest down the end of the pit lane because they had been sent for the crew to be doing fitness exercises. The van had arrived late so we had to unpack it at the top of the paddock and move kettle bells and air con units on a wheelie tray an hour before the session in extreme heat.

'You just have to adapt and deal with it. It could be marketing kit, car parts, it could be someone had forgotten their trainers. Once the race weekend starts, anything that turns up is our responsibility, whether it is to do with us or not.'

Transport in the opposite direction is also required, it transpires, and as the weekend comes to a close and the pack-up process begins, even that sometimes represents a requirement for Lacy-Smith to think on her feet. 'Sending bits back is also down to us, including whatever the drivers have been given during the race,' she says. 'So often in the middle of pack-up trying to get everything into the vans or into freight, one of the marketing team will say, "This driver's been given this picture. Can you get it safely back to the factory?" And we have to try and do our best. In Japan they always get big models and they all have to go back to the factory.'

It is an addition to a pack-up process that is physically demanding and all the while also requires concentration on component management. At race close she will help with the tyres first, getting all the rims out of the bags, bagging up all the covers and helping out until the cars come back. At which point they make sure the mechanics have their servicing lists, so they can get every part off the car that can't do the next race.

Any damage on the car would also have been recorded and a list sent back to the factory while also packing up any requests for parts that the factory wanted sent back, whether for modification or testing, or anything that is not needed any more.

This is no short process on what is a long day. It is around six to seven hours after the race has finished that Lacy-Smith will leave the track and she has only ever once walked out before nightfall.

On flyaways especially she concedes it can all be something of a challenge. 'You can be working in thirty-degree-plus heat, or five-degree cold, and you have to just deal with that,' she says. 'You have to learn to cope with the elements. We tend to be out the back of the garage in quite a lot of races. In Russia it was hailing and we just had the barest cover above us and it was cold and windy, making it difficult to do your job.'

Yet for all that, her satisfaction, pleasure and pride at being a part of it, having made it to the top of that automotive industry that had sparked her imagination in a car showroom, is impossible to ignore, even if her work remains hidden from view.

'F1 is very different in reality; there is so much more than what you see on the telly,' she says with a smile. 'There is so much more around it, so much more you would never ever see from the outside. Sometimes, when you are on your knees in the garage bubble-wrapping parts at 10 p.m. at night on a Sunday, you think, "What am I doing here?" But really, deep down, you know you enjoy it and that's why we keep doing it.'

CHAPTER 15

THE TECHNICIAN

JACK PARTRIDGE
GARAGE TECHNICIAN – ASTON MARTIN ARAMCO
COGNIZANT F1 TEAM

'Once a race gets going, I am in the garage; it's all set up but until we get one pit-stop done I am still absolutely bricking it. Once we have done that, I know everything is working and operational. Even to this day I get nervous that something has gone wrong.'

Some roles have been a fundamental part of F1 for so long they have left an indelible impression. One is woven into the history, to the very fabric of the sport such that for all that it has changed over time, it remains an essential part of the modern operation. Aston Martin's Jack Partridge then is officially a garage technician, but he and his colleagues across the paddock are known with affection as 'truckies'. It is a pleasing anachronism since the one task they no longer actually do is drive trucks, yet while the nickname will stick forever it belies a complex and vital part of every team.

The term truckies, as the name suggests, originated from the drivers of the trucks that would transport the cars and team equipment to races. When F1 was a simpler affair they were masters of a multifaceted trade. Climbing behind the wheel to take the gear to the track and, upon arrival, unpacking the equipment, the cars, building the garage and then setting about a myriad of tasks over a race weekend before packing it all away again at the end, then once more taking the wheel to move on to the next race or returning home.

In a sense they were a jack of all trades from the days when teams might take only one or two trucks to a race. Their legacy lives on in the garage technician who must also be ready to turn their hand to anything, not least in what is referred to colourfully across the paddock as a 'shit fight'. The all-hands-on-deck moment, often crash-induced, which Partridge positively revels in, at odds no doubt with the anguished pain felt by the accountants back at base.

'I am sure some mechanics would admit that those moments, when they have to throw themselves into a job against the clock and against the odds, showing just how well we can all work together, is exciting and it's good to get involved with,' he says. 'Like Monaco in 2022 when Lance Stroll hit the barrier and broke a gearbox at the Swimming Pool chicane. We had a gearbox swap going on with Sebastian Vettel's car as well. I jumped on to help the mechanics out. There was stuff going everywhere but I know how to put a nut and bolt together.

It's absolute carnage in the garage but it's pretty exhilarating, especially when you get the car out again having changed the gearbox in an hour and a half. What a feeling.'

Nowadays a team will be transporting approximately 32 tons of equipment for flyaway meetings, including four containers of garage equipment transported via sea freight to each one. In Europe it is moved by around twenty-nine trucks, nine for race equipment and twenty for hospitality, such is the palatial splendour demanded in the modern era. With the sheer volume of equipment and the punishing F1 schedule, including triple- and double-header meetings, unsurprisingly the actual driving of the trucks has long been outsourced to specialized companies, but when the gear arrives the teams take over.

The twenty-seven-year-old has been with Aston Martin since he joined them when they were Force India in 2018. He has no issues with his profession's nickname. 'Garage technician is effectively what they used to call a truckie but without the driving of the trucks,' he says with a smile. 'The nickname is still "the truckie" but I don't mind.'

Partridge enjoys his job, regardless of title, and it is impossible not to sense the pleasure the young man takes from his task in F1, because he has found a place within a sport he always dreamed of joining, even if it is not quite as he imagined it as a youngster.

A talented karter, as with many in the sport, he had harboured hopes of driving at the top, but any place in F1 was a goal that felt beyond reach when real life impinged and he went to work on a building site after leaving school. Little wonder then that travelling the world as part of the Aston Martin team gives this cheerful, optimistic young man reason to feel a sense of achievement.

Partridge grew up in rural Suffolk and took to karting at the indoor track his grandad owned in Ipswich. It was very much a family venue, his father met his mother there and their son remembers going when he was as young as four. 'They used to get the marshals to push me round the track because I couldn't reach the pedals,' he says. Meanwhile at home, Dad ensured he was also watching history being made.

'My biggest memory of F1 then was coming down to watch it on a Sunday with my dad who is a Ferrari fan,' Partridge recalls. 'Watching Michael Schumacher in the early 2000s winning everything and Dad was on the sofa cheering him on. My dad was the big link to F1; he was why I got interested in it.' Dad's influence ultimately paid off and made him proud.

When Partridge could reach the pedals at the kart track it turned out he had quite the touch. He started racing when he was nine and moved on to the British Championship. He finished eighth when he was ten years old, continued progressing through junior categories and went on to win the British Junior Championship when he was fifteen in 2012. At the time he was managed by Alex Hawkridge, the former principal of the Toleman F1 team who could spot a good driver when he saw one, having signed Ayrton Senna to the team in 1984.

He described Partridge's 'dedication, sacrifice and burning ambition to succeed as a professional racing driver', summing up well a driver who was without doubt committed to his goal. 'I always wanted to get into F1,' he says, of those heady days. 'But I tried to be realistic about it. I just wanted a successful career driving in motorsport but the dream was always to be an F1 driver.'

Indeed with the optimism of youth, and what is now no little sense of irony, he had not even considered there was a career in the sport beyond the cockpit. 'I didn't even think about being in F1 as anything other than a driver,' he says. 'When my engine builder for karting offered me the opportunity to go and learn how he built the engines and how it all worked, I remember saying stupidly at the time: "Why do I want to do that? I drive the car, I don't need to know how it works." It never crossed my mind until later on in life that you could be in F1 as something other than a driver.'

The almost inevitable intervention of the brutal reality of going racing put paid to this youthful ambition. He made it as far as a test in single seaters before the costs became prohibitive. The sponsors and backing he had hoped for after the British karting title did not materialize and after only a year on a minimal budget in senior karting, the money ran out and his dreams made haste for the exit in its wake. The story is familiar to drivers across the sport, nowadays more than ever.

'Reality hit. I was leaving school, I needed a job, life suddenly hit me and I had to go out and start working,' he says. 'The dream faded out. I ended up working on a building site for a couple of years. The motorsport career was dead. It was a shock, disappointing, when everything just stops; you are not racing at all and you are suddenly working.'

Beyond driving, Partridge had made no plans for the future. He was not academic – more hands-on than pen and paper as he describes it – and had no desire to try to go to university, and building work may have loomed large for the future but for a serendipitous meeting.

At eighteen in 2016 he had been asked to drive again for a season in senior karting, having kept as involved as he could with driver coaching. While racing he met Marcus Smith, who worked at Pirelli fitting tyres for F1 and F2. 'We did a charity kart race together and one day he told me a job had come up at Pirelli,' Partridge explains. 'I had never fitted a tyre in my life outside of karts, but I applied and got the job.

'When that opportunity came, that was the first time I thought I could have a career in F1 but not as a driver, as a technician. I had left school, left karting, not knowing what I would do.'

Fate had been kind and, with pleasing happenstance, Smith is also now a garage technician at Mercedes.

Partridge recognized this as a big chance and joined Pirelli as a tyre fitter in F2 and F3 learning the trade as he went, fitting the tyres, taking temperatures, ensuring the correct sets are ready, stripping them off the rims. He adapted to the full gamut with such alacrity that he was moved to the F1 Pirelli team the next year. This was a new experience again but one he revelled in and recognized as offering even more opportunities. He made use of it, finding out how the teams operated and working with garage technicians, so when a job as one came up at Force India he applied and was once more successful.

Four-and-a-half years after joining the building trade he was at the heart of an F1 team, a development he had not expected. 'I think I did get lucky but I have never been a great believer in needing to go to university and getting a degree,' he says. 'I left school when I was sixteen and I got lucky in the contact at Pirelli, but I think you make your own luck a little bit.'

This was a life-changing turning point that a few short years previously had been unthinkable, a moment as unexpected as it was welcome. 'It was massive,' he recalls. 'By that point I knew I was never going to make it as a driver so it was the next best thing. I hadn't achieved the dream but it was better than working on a building site,' he laughs, before revealing that it also went down really well at home. 'My dad was most excited,' he says. 'As time goes on for me, the job became the norm; day-to-day working in F1 is normal life, but to my dad every day, he is still excited about it.'

It was something of a baptism of fire for the young man, however. He knew the basics of the job. That there were between four and six garage technicians on a team and they were there to build, maintain and look after the equipment in the garage and the garage itself, alongside becoming an extra pair of arms and legs as circumstances might dictate.

'I was thrown straight into the race team at the deep end,' he says. 'I had to learn everything from how to build garage panels to maintaining and using equipment. My main role is to look after the pit-stop gantry but there is so much to take in: the way the trucks operate, the way everything is loaded, how the equipment works, how things go together, the operations of the team day to day through the week. I am still learning now.'

On race weekend the teams have a set-up crew that arrive on the Saturday before the race who build up the basics from a bare garage using a plan of how it should be, drawn specifically for every circuit. This is necessary because while from the outside the garages around the world may appear largely uniform, it is an illusion created by careful and adroit management of the garage panels – the shiny plastic boards that convert unwelcoming bare concrete walls into a polished corporate sheen that form the workspace.

The reality is that every venue is different. From Monaco where the garage stretches vertically over three floors to the cavernous open spaces of Silverstone. They must adapt to different electrical plans and to a plethora of varying layouts and facilities. Behind the scenes then it is an improvised workspace, unique to every venue, but designed to be as similar and crucially as familiar as possible such that it feels at home for the crew.

This is most evident in what is known as the horseshoe – the front of the garage where the cars sit. This space is designed to be virtually identical every race, so the cars and mechanics have the same amount of space, equipment is instinctively in exactly the same place, distances between items can be measured and defined by muscle memory.

When the garage technicians arrive on a Tuesday, walkways are defined, the lights are up, the panels are up, as are the pods that sit above the car that gives mechanics airline connections, power and lights to work on the car. The framework there, ready to be filled.

Partridge and his colleagues then begin by unloading the air freight: the cars, the toolboxes, all the equipment required for the weekend. Each has a specific responsibility: one on the timing stand and fuel side, one an electrician, one working with the tyre crew from Pirelli, one floating technician to help the others where needed and one with Partridge's personal responsibility, the pit-stop equipment.

He builds the pit-stop gantry on a Wednesday as the mechanics arrive to build the car. The gantry is the mechanical boom system that projects out in front of the garage to hang over the cars' pit box. It is an absolutely vital part of the equipment. It supports the airlines that power the wheel guns – connected to air bottles pressured to a fearsome 300 bar – and the front and rear jacks, all of which hang off the boom and without which the two-and-a-half-second pit-stop that is now the norm would be but a fantasy. There are complex electrical connections too that feed the assortment of sensors embedded in the wheel gun and jacks to ensure that a car can safely be released.

It is an immensely complicated piece of equipment, one where failure or malfunction would be enormously costly during a stop and Partridge takes his responsibilities understandably seriously.

'Once it is all up and running there is not a lot you need to do to the systems through a session,' he says. 'But once a race gets going I am sitting there in the garage – it's all set up; there's nothing I need to do to the system, but until we get one pit-stop done I am absolutely bricking it. Once we have done that stop I know everything is working and operational even though I have checked it 100 times. Even to this day I get nervous that something has gone wrong, we have sprung a leak or had an electrical failure. It hasn't happened yet, touch wood.'

With the gantry in place, ready for pit-stop practice which can begin as early as 10 a.m. on a Thursday, Partridge will help out in a multitude of tasks, including helping the tyre crew process and getting ready all the sets of tyres or preparing equipment such as the grid trolleys, all the while keeping an eye on the sensitive gantry gear. But he also has two other major roles to complete. On Friday during practice he is one of the two crew in charge of refuelling. Working on Lance Stroll's car he is usually responsible for the fire extinguisher, standing next to the refueller in case anything goes wrong while the fuel is going in. Meanwhile in between fuelling he fills in where needed in the garage.

Being clear of set-up work by Thursday is also vital in his other role as a member of the pit crew. Partridge is responsible for putting on the right front wheel on both cars during pit-stops, so when pit-stop practice begins, he is at its heart. During this intimidating, high-pressure dance it is he who lifts and bangs on the wheel with fresh rubber, a task that must be achieved perfectly in microseconds. It was, somewhat surprisingly, another role that he had to be on top of in no short order.

'It's a great, active role I have had since I started,' he says. 'On my first race weekend I was on the pit crew, and it was exciting, nerve-wracking, all the emotions rolled into one. We do so much practice but five years on it is still such an exciting part of the job, yet it also becomes second nature because I have done so many pit-stops.'

Saturday, with the business end of the weekend coming into play at qualifying, the tension ratchets up with Partridge once more on the extinguisher and monitoring anything that needs doing in the garage.

'The most intense session of the weekend is qualifying by a long shot because it is such a tight time constraint,' he says. 'The engineers push it as tight as they can to get as much track time as they can and that puts more strain on the garage. But we have a great routine, and we gel well as a team. People are concentrating on the job but we are calm. As soon as the car rolls out of the garage, everyone relaxes, we can have a laugh and a joke, take in a breath.'

The next day, five hours before the off, he will arrive at the track on Sunday. It's early on what will be a very long day. However, with no track running before the start it is an easier morning, with time to check every detail, every piece of equipment in the garage, for the tyres to be readied in the correct order as expected by the engineers for the stops, that the tyre and wing change gear is in the right place and that constant, overriding responsibility looming larger now than ever, that everything on the gantry is absolutely shipshape.

With it deployed successfully – and in five years of hawkish care, Partridge has still yet to have a problem with it during a race – and having played his part on the right-front during the pit-stops, the end is in sight, but the serious business for the garage tech is just beginning: the pack-up.

It is all but impossible to witness this and not be astounded by the breathtaking rapidity with which it occurs. It is a balletic, choreographed dance of men, women and machinery, often inches apart, acting in concert with both unfeasible precision and at pace. For Partridge this is where the adrenaline really flows.

'That's when I say the real race starts,' he says. 'Everyone wants to get packed up as quickly as possible, so it is full on. The flag drops, everyone jumps out of their suits and unless you have had a good result – a podium, or it is the end of the season – everyone is straight on to crack on with their work.

'I am taking everything apart on the pit-stop gantry; everything we used for a pit-stop – which takes a day to put together – I have taken apart in forty-five minutes. Me and three of the crew jump on it and forty-five minutes later the pit lane is cleared of equipment. It's packed, it's boxed and ready to be loaded into the air freight pallets.'

The full pack-up, including the mechanics stripping the car down, takes between four and five hours in Europe and around six in the flyaway rounds during which, if they are lucky, there may be about twenty minutes at some point to snaffle some grub.

Long after the glamour boys have left the circuit on private planes, the hard graft carries on for these unsung heroes. 'There is just loads going on,' he explains. 'Freight being packed at the back of the garage, air freight being packed at the front, mechanics trying to strip the cars, while stores and chief mechanics organize all the parts being thrown at them from the mechanics. It is intense and I get quite a buzz out of actually packing up. I know it's an odd thing to say. I know a lot of people hate it, but I get a buzz out of getting it done as quickly as possible, just smashing it out.'

It ends a long weekend before the flight home on Monday, in what is clearly an enormously satisfying role for Partridge. The irrepressible truckie taking pleasure in success on the track for the team, but also in a great pit-stop and in having executed his role successfully all weekend as part of what is an exceptionally well-oiled but also a pleasingly exuberant machine.

'You have to be very focused of course,' he says. 'But what you become very good at as a team is you can be talking, be having a laugh and a joke, but as soon as something comes over the radio, everyone is gone, straight to their jobs, knowing exactly what has to be done. Everyone is very good at switching between work and being able to relax, but when it gets down to the nitty gritty, everyone is really on it.'

CHAPTER 16

THE ACADEMY HEAD

GUILLAUME ROCQUELIN
HEAD OF DRIVER ACADEMY - ORACLE RED BULL RACING

'I worked with David Coulthard a year after starting at Red Bull Racing, then Sebastian Vettel, Daniel Ricciardo, Daniil Kvyat, Pierre Gasly and of course Max Verstappen. All different characters, different personalities and that lets me paint a picture of a driver as an athlete and as a human being, and I bring that to the academy drivers. You can see what they are good at, what strengths they have and what they are missing because you have seen it before.'

Guillaume Rocquelin is best known by his nickname 'Rocky', a moniker under which he came to be recognized globally as the race engineer who helped steer Sebastian Vettel and then Max Verstappen to Drivers' Championships. In the process he has gained experience second to none, working with world champions and a team at the very sharp end of the sport. Little wonder then that Red Bull Racing turned to him when they were looking for a leader to forge the next generation of potentially title-winning drivers.

Rocquelin is as enthusiastic about the challenge with these young chargers as he ever was with Vettel and Verstappen. He worked with Vettel as race engineer for six years, delivering carefully controlled communication, speaking in English gently accented by his native French, over the German's radio. This voice of reason, of advice, of warning and of eager encouragement made him publicly well known as he helped Vettel take four titles between 2010 and 2013. His was a calming presence when required, and also one of consolation and of celebration that demonstrated the close bond the two had formed.

Rocquelin was shifted to become head of race engineering in 2015 and was at the helm there when Verstappen won his first title in 2021 before he decided to step back from the front line to take on a new challenge with up-and-coming talent. He had developed a taste for this – the challenge of extracting the maximum from man rather than machine – in his time with Vettel, and relished applying it to the next generation.

'As an engineer, at a certain point you know the car is only so good,' he says. 'Then you realize there is untapped potential by working with a driver and seeing them develop, to become the best they can be, and that is very interesting. Having been through different profiles of drivers, I had an understanding of the strengths and weaknesses in becoming a good F1 driver. Now it gives me the urge to get up every morning because you get to meet fifteen- to twenty-year-old drivers and they are just hungry; they want it so badly. That's how I was in my own way twenty years ago – it was all about racing.'

Rocquelin joined Red Bull in 2006, the team's second season in the sport, as a test and third-car engineer, and in 2007 became race engineer to David Coulthard. There was, he stresses, no sense at all of the inevitability of success at the team, no indication of the scale of glory that was to come. He notes that at the time, seventh in the championship was their level and it was hard to imagine much more.

Progression, however, was the target and he and they kept plugging away. Even in 2010, their first title year, he admits Red Bull did not see it coming, perhaps unsurprisingly given that Vettel had not led the championship at all until the flag fell on the decisive last race in Abu Dhabi, a result of such weight he reveals it took some time to even digest that it had happened.

What followed was a roller coaster, not least in that Rocquelin worked at the top of the sport with two of the modern era's greatest talents. Indeed, he is one of the very few people in F1 to be able to learn from and draw close, first-hand comparisons between Vettel and Verstappen, a process that has informed his role today.

'Max was a very different profile to Sebastian; his approach, his skill set,' he explains. 'Max's confidence is incredible. His skills are a generational talent; there is no doubt about that.

Sebastian spent a lot more time with the engineers trying to get the detail.

'Now, as an engineer, it's easy to say the right way to get on is to work hard with a methodology, to try to understand all the details, to write notes and prepare notes and have a very organized approach to racing. Then you get to work with somebody like Max who just comes in and says, "Yeah, don't worry I will just get it done," and, well, actually he does.

'It makes you reconsider what you think is right and how you should approach things. You learn a lot – there might not just be one way of skinning the cat. You have to respect other people's way of looking at things, at their talent, how they get the job done, so of course you keep on learning.'

Unassuming, immediately friendly and open, with an expansive and intimate knowledge of the sport, it is hard to imagine Rocquelin in any other profession. Yet for some time a career in F1 seemed entirely unlikely, a journey he did not even countenance while growing up entirely oblivious to motor racing.

The fifty-four-year-old was born in Dijon in Burgundy, France, to a family with no interest in motor racing, a sport he describes as quite alien to his parents at the time. Indeed, in 1979 when home-grown French driver Jean-Pierre Jabouille took French team Renault's first victory in F1 at the Dijon-Prenois track, a race that also featured that glorious wheel-banging battle between René Arnoux and Gilles Villeneuve, young Rocky was unaware it was even happening, despite the circuit being only ten miles from his house.

Rocquelin only went to Dijon to see some racing when he was eighteen, having had his head finally turned by watching the 1984 Monaco Grand Prix, where Alain Prost won under a red flag in the wet and Ayrton Senna gave notice of his exceptional talent, driving the wheels off his Toleman.

Yet his decision to then pursue a career in racing was not one of simple enthusiasm sparked by racing, but a reflection of the satisfaction he felt might be derived from having a definitive measure against which to test himself.

'When I was starting to take my A levels I was trying to figure out what to do with my career; I was trying to figure out what jobs there were,' he says. 'I was quite interested in science but also in not having a nine-to-five job. The main attraction for me was that I was really keen to have some kind of tangible proof of the work I did.

'So having something that comes every two weeks, where you have to race and you have a very clear classification in the results that shows how you are performing was quite gratifying compared to a regular job. Then I saw Monaco, the cars, the spectacle of that captured my imagination. So I put it all together and I thought, "There is a career there," so I made my plans around being part of that world.'

At which point Rocquelin opted to pursue engineering and the long undertaking of higher education, including specialist engineering school in France to earn that coveted title, something he felt was a challenge that suited his character. 'I never fancied being a driver. I am not a very good driver and I wouldn't want to put myself out there to compete against others,' he says. 'It is a personal challenge as an engineer. I am reasonably introverted, so it's not like I want to be challenging people. It's more a personal satisfaction of a job well done I like pursuing.'

In the 1980s, even while Renault were making a mark in F1, it was rallying which was huge in France, with Peugeot one of the leading teams. Rocquelin had thus far expressed no particular preference of which discipline he might pursue in his career in motorsport, and he recalls he may well have gone into rallying but for a chance intercession by John Steed and Emma Peel.

'What swung it for me regarding it being F1 was Gérard Ducarouge,' he says.

'Gérard was a French engineer, was technical director at Lotus and I remember seeing this article where he was working in his office at their base in Hethel in Norfolk. It was honestly like watching *The Avengers* in terms of the decor of the thing, of this small group of people working on these really tricky cars and going to race them against the world. It appealed to me more than working in a muddy field I have to say. F1 was a bit more James Bond than rallying ...'

Having qualified as an engineer, Rocquelin went to work with the UK manufacturer Reynard as a designer on their CART/IndyCar programme before moving on to take a role for them as a race engineer with teams in the US. There he worked with Mark Blundell at the PacWest team before moving on to Newman/Haas. It was a period he cites as invaluable in learning the trade. The set-up on the cars in IndyCar can be changed in the pit lane because they are built to be easy and accessible, while the tyres at the time were very durable so degradation was not a factor. All this facilitates a process of testing and adaptation in rapid progression at the track, as well as a steep learning curve for the fledgling engineer.

Rocquelin stayed in the States for six years before stepping up to F1, joining the new British American Racing team in

1999, their first year in the sport. While the culmination of an ambition, reaching the pinnacle of racing was, he acknowledges, a major new challenge.

'The step between motor racing in general and F1 is massive and it is getting bigger every day,' he says. 'When you look at the F1 car, it is a space rocket. The Indy car is a great race car and I really enjoyed working with it, but it is functional and basic. I have a lot of respect and time for IndyCar but in terms of being able to do everything to the nth degree, where cost is not a limit, practicality is not a limit, F1 is just something else. The F1 car is so much lighter, so much quicker; everything is designed with no compromise whatsoever. It was a different beast, a big eye-opener.'

For all that it was a major step up, the time in the US had been invaluable in allowing Rocquelin to hone his craft such that when he arrived at Red Bull he was able to focus on making a difference to a very human component: the man behind the wheel.

'Those years at IndyCar made me a good technical race engineer, through testing and experience,' he explains. 'But in F1 you become more of a specialist, then you really focus to work one-to-one with a driver. You know that everything else is 100 per cent and what you are left with is working with the driver to improve that.'

He did so in exemplary fashion for the next sixteen seasons at Red Bull before deciding that a change was in order for 2022. Having been in racing for thirty years, he felt there was little more he could give to, or take from, the engineer role.

'Because I like learning and developing myself I was trying to expand my knowledge, but because of that repetition after so long in F1 I wanted a different challenge,' he says.

The driver academy concept developed from young driver programmes and has now been a staple in F1 for more than two decades. Every team boasts an academy in some form or another according to the scale of their ability to invest in young talent, and they are an increasingly vital part of any team's armoury. Vettel came through Red Bull's programme, Lewis Hamilton as part of McLaren's and Charles Leclerc through Ferrari's.

They are a proving ground to identify the talent of the future and the competition to pick up the best young drivers among teams is fierce. No one wants to miss out on the next Hamilton or Verstappen. Red Bull were, alongside Alpine, earlier adopters, one of the first to instigate a young driver programme in the early 2000s, and have seen a range of drivers come up through their ranks. Originally this process would be largely based around providing backing for drivers, enabling them to progress in a sport where funding can make or break careers.

However, that has since evolved into the far more hands-on approach of the academy, a dedicated set-up within a team to address every aspect of what is required to be a successful driver nowadays, and in so doing ensure the juniors have the best possible chance to make the most of their talent.

Red Bull has retained its junior team, a sponsorship programme putting promising drivers in teams, but it now runs in tandem with the academy, which is a broader, more wide-ranging project where Rocquelin takes the reins to guide the next generation.

Each year Rocquelin receives a list of the candidates from Red Bull's director of motorsport, Helmut Marko, the former driver who has overseen the team's driver development programme and is adept at spotting new talent. They are inducted into the academy where they take part in simulator sessions and classroom courses, they interact with the team and are brought up to speed with Red Bull's values and operational structures and methods. They attend tests, observe operations room support and meet the F1 drivers to get a feel for where they are and where they might be in future.

There are usually between eight and twelve drivers inducted each year. The short-term aim is to have them perform as best they can in their current racing categories, but also to have them best placed should they go further.

Every element is geared towards improving the young drivers' abilities overall, not just behind the wheel. They will be expected to gain an understanding of team briefings, how they work and why they are vital, to acknowledge and address fitness and dietary needs and to grasp a level of technical understanding. Courses are tailored to their needs, such as vehicle dynamics and aerodynamics, to ensure an understanding of how suspension works, how the wings work in order to be able to interact on a meaningful level with engineers. It is a comprehensive and essential process, both educational and technical, and they will regularly spend their time between races at Red Bull Racing's Technology Campus in Milton Keynes.

These budding future stars arrive ranging in age from when they are allowed by law to drive cars in their home country. In the UK that is fifteen years old for British Formula 4. They may be signed a year earlier in karting, giving them a chance to get ahead on single seaters by doing sim time before they step up to the real thing. If they make the course, they will stay in the academy until they reach what Rocquelin calls the 'doors of F1' as twenty or twenty-one-year-olds in Formula 2.

Rocquelin emphasizes that every academy entrant is identified first and foremost for their driving talent. 'They are all in the programme because they are all seen as potential F1 race winners, otherwise they would not be there,' he says. However, once on board he stresses that expectations are high beyond just performing on track and that managing young people in such a daunting and intense environment is a singular task.

'We can't be blinkered and say, "You will be fine, do your own thing." We have to be objective and honest but there must also be a sense of safeguarding because we are dealing with children not adults, and you have to be really careful about that as well,' he explains. 'The expectations from a fifteen-year-old are different from somebody going into F2 and expecting to win the championship. That is something we looked at by working with football academies in understanding how you manage younger athletes. You have to respect the growth process physically and mentally. At fifteen you will not have the same make-up as a twenty-year-old.

'So, in Formula 4 mistakes are expected because it is part of the learning process. If they make mistakes early in their careers it is an opportunity to learn, so we reward that and we look forward to that, because we found something they didn't know and through that they are becoming a better driver. But if you get to F2 going for the championship, mistakes will start to not be tolerated and that will be explained to them.'

During pre-season, the onus is on simulator work. Preparing the drivers for circuits, familiarizing them with the environments, rehearsing the weekends for qualifying and racing. Intriguingly, Rocquelin describes the simulator as like using a gym, a process of getting his charges to race fitness in terms of learning their craft.

Later in the season the emphasis is much more on understanding how their chosen sport works, including an immersion within the F1 facilities at every level. They will be coming to the Red Bull Technology Campus to work in the workshop, to work in the paint shop, going to the ops room to watch races unfold and observe how they are handled back at base. It is a comprehensive interaction with the extensive array of people and roles that make up a team and the support they provide that is so vital to the drivers at the sharp end on a Sunday.

Running it all is, to an extent, a world away from where Rocquelin's career began and one he admits is an altogether different challenge. Now he must not only build relationships but also take care in delineating them with these budding young drivers – a fine but vital line to walk.

'It's really important to generate trust and respect,' he says. 'But I am very mindful to be objective and unbiased. Which means that whatever interaction we have, it has to be based on very clear facts and honesty.'

He elaborates, describing how they cannot allow the relationship to become too familiar or casual, but rather requires a pact on behalf of everyone involved.

'At the start of the year I lay out the things I am expecting of them in terms of behaviour and expectations, and then what they are going to get out of the programme,' he says. 'It's like a deal of what they have to do and what I have to do. The way

I treat this is very much based on honesty and clarity, but I am very cautious in not becoming their friend. That is not the idea. I am a mentor, or coach, or teacher and they are here to learn. I expect them to respect the information I pass on but that is it.'

These kids do not lack for motivation; that is certain. No one underestimates what an enormous chance they are being offered in an F1 academy and being taken under Rocky's wing is a privilege they know must be seized. 'The fact that I have quite a bit of experience and I like to think I know what I am talking about also helps a lot,' he says with a smile.

Rocquelin enjoyed a huge professional and personal satisfaction in the first half of his career. With Vettel and then Verstappen he has been at the very heart of some of the greatest moments F1 can possibly offer, tasted the ultimate level of success, of victory in fierce competition under intense pressure. Yet it is not beyond compare for the engineer, who has found a new appreciation from passing on all the hard lessons learned along the way.

'The biggest kick I get out of the academy is when you have a driver who struggles through something,' he says. 'You sit down with them, go through it, train with them, you measure improvement and then they go to the next race and win it. What a feeling, to pass on some knowledge, realize it makes a difference and somebody has been able to grow through it? Just fantastic.'

CHAPTER 17

THE CHIEF MECHANIC

KARI LAMMENRANTA
CHIEF MECHANIC - MCLAREN FORMULA 1 TEAM

'I never harboured any thoughts of ever working in Formula One, that was beyond a farm boy's grasp. After secondary school my occupational training was as a house builder. I was never formally trained as a car mechanic. I have learned it all on the job, through the smaller formulas that were my apprenticeship, right up to F1, and I am still learning now.'

Across the two cars each F1 team fields every race weekend at the track, they are built, managed, repaired and run by the loving ministrations of around fifteen to twenty mechanics. The majority of them, with their sleeves rolled up getting stuck into the innards of the car, or delicately adjusting the tiniest components, or with their hands on wheels and guns during pit-stops, are known as number two mechanics. Each side of the garage then has its own number one mechanic who oversees the crews for each car. Presiding over and organizing this complex, highly skilled collection of personnel at the very sharp end of making an F1 car run is the conductor of that orchestra, the chief mechanic.

At McLaren, Kari Lammenranta is the man holding the baton and in the twenty-one years he has been with the team he has fulfilled every one of the mechanic roles to reach the point where he is now responsible for all of them. Moreover, it has been all but a lifelong journey, an experience and an education that he still occasionally finds hard to quite come to terms with. Not at all bad for the farm boy from Finland.

The forty-eight-year-old still speaks with a Finnish accent, and a smile that often becomes a big, beaming infectious grin, indicating indisputably that he still enjoys what he does even after so long. His pride and pleasure is matched by the value of his enormous experience in coming through the ranks, where you learn an awful lot on the way, as illustrated when he recalls his time as a number two mechanic and was engaged in the complete set of tasks during pit-stops.

'I started at the left rear-on and then went to front gun, then to rear gun, then I went back to left front-on,' he says. 'Now I know what everyone is doing in a pit-stop because I have done it myself. That is important, especially understanding the gun job, knowing what they need to do. Even now when I am not doing it I can actually hear whether everything went well or not in a pit-stop. That's because I have worked through all these roles to reach this position.'

They were skills that were hard-earned the old-fashioned way and over no short period of time. Indeed it is such a fascinating and in some ways almost unlikely a story, it deserves to be given full rein.

Lammenranta was born in south-west Finland where he grew up on a small dairy farm near the town of Salo. There was no motorsport tradition in the family unless, as Lammenranta notes with a grin, you counted racing tractors.

The young Lammenranta's introduction to the sport was in fact one of those lucky moments of chance that it transpires have repeatedly shaped his life. 'It was in the era of Keke Rosberg in 1986 when I saw an F1 race for the first time on TV; it was Monaco,' he recalls. 'My dad explained it to me and I got quite interested so I started watching it more and more. Basically it was by accident I saw it on TV, yet there was something that started a fascination in me about it.'

It was the first of a series of events, largely unplanned, as Lammenranta simply followed his nose that would ultimately lead to McLaren and F1. After concluding his army service, he was considering what to do next when fate intervened and characteristically he decided to simply go with the flow.

'I came out of the army and there weren't many jobs going because of the recession,' he says. 'I met up with an old friend and he knew someone into racing who was trying to start his own team in Germany. He was starting a Formula Opel team. So I asked him if he needed anybody. I hadn't had any experience of Formula cars at that point but, well he got me a plane ticket, so I went to Frankfurt.'

There was both romance and rationale in just following his instinct to this as he explains. 'Being a farm boy, I was playing with tractors and machinery so I knew quite a lot about how engines and cars work and liked that,' he says. 'I also thought, "Yes, I get out of Finland for the first time in my life and I get to learn something that is quite interesting to me." I was in my early twenties and racing cars were something I wanted to have a look at, so why not?'

Yet really it was very much a leap into the unknown. 'I had never met this guy before, he was a friend of friend, so I was taking a chance,' he says. 'Also Formula Opel were pretty bad racing cars to be honest. It worked out well at first but we only did a few races then it didn't quite work out at that team, but it had made me want more.'

He returned to Finland and hunted down the British motor racing magazine *Autosport*, then hard to find in his home country, looking for the appointments that were advertised in the publication. He duly found a job in England working with Renault Spiders, which was also short-lived, but stuck to the task. His friend had moved to Belgium to join a Formula 3000 team and once more Lammenranta went with the flow.

'My friend said there is a place here so off I went,' he says with pleasing insouciance. 'I met a guy from the team at a train station who had been picking something up from the UK and he took me to Belgium. Thinking about it now there were a lot of things that went correct: the timings were right, right place, right time. Things just fell into place.'

The team he joined in 1997 in F3000 was Astromega and Lammenranta would learn much of his trade with them over the next six years, during which time double world champion Fernando Alonso would race for them in the year 2000. It was invaluable to the young mechanic as he soaked up the skills and tricks of the trade from his more experienced colleagues at Astromega.

'I was a mechanic, a rear-ender to start with,' says Lammenranta. 'After three years, in 2000, I made it to become a number one mechanic to run one of the cars. I picked it up quickly but you are only as good as your teachers. I was still an apprentice at first, and you have to listen and follow what they tell you because racing cars are very different to road cars.

'Some of it I felt came naturally but some of it didn't. Some things I didn't quite understand but after a while you start getting it. Why things are done in a certain way. You wonder why we are going into it in such detail, but after a while you understand it because that is what you have to do with a racing car.'

This understanding of the importance of attention to detail, of structure, of a strictly organized methodology and approach are paramount in racing and more so than ever in F1, where the margins are impossibly small and errors or inattention have competitive and even dangerous consequences.

Lammenranta wanted to develop as he learned but had to adapt perhaps quicker than he might have thought. On a skiing holiday in January 2003, Astromega's manager warned him the team were considering stopping racing and they ultimately called it a day in F3000 the following year. So Lammenranta came off the slopes to consider his options now that racing was definitely in the blood. It was a turning point, a divergence that saw him step up in racing's pecking order rather than treading water. Once more he was in the right place at the right time.

'A friend said they were advertising for McLaren and Williams who wanted staff,' he says. 'At that point I knew someone who worked in McLaren so I called him and he spoke to Indy Lall who was the test team manager at that time in March 2003. He said, "Send in your CV." So I did that, and a couple of days later I went for an interview and I got the job. It was as a number two mechanic on test team three.'

Lall was already a veteran at McLaren having started with the team in 1981. He had been Alain Prost's number one mechanic during the Frenchman's title-winning season in 1986. Today he manages McLaren's heritage events department, including their magnificent collection of former race cars.

Clearly recognizing potential in Lammenranta, Lall gave him a shot on the third test team, a luxury that has long since disappeared from F1. Back then, with unrestricted testing and no budget caps, teams would have two test teams and associated crew to assess the cars and engines and a third just for tyre testing, known at the time after the tyre manufacturer as the Michelin car. Which is where Lammenranta got his break on the McLaren MP4-17D, driven the previous season by David Coulthard and Lammenranta's fellow Finn, Kimi Raikkonen.

With the history, the success, the scale of the team and its position at the very cutting edge of F1, it was a huge moment for him. Understandably it remains indelibly imprinted on his mind as he could scarcely believe it was happening with not a little sensation of imposter syndrome.

'It was 12 April 2003 – that was my first day,' he says. 'Don't print this but I shit myself that first day. When you come to a company like this, you know its background and you think, "What am I doing here?" "Am I supposed to be here?" "Am I in the right place?" An F3000 team is a maximum of ten people and one car crew then at McLaren was ten people. It took a while to get my head around it that I was working for the McLaren F1 team.'

He had started, aptly, where the team itself had begun, at the team's famous Unit 22. Two years after Bruce McLaren had formed the team in 1963, they had moved to this unassuming business park in Colnbrook and it was from there until 1981 they built a motor racing legend. The team had moved to larger premises in Woking in 1981 but had kept the historic factory and it was where the tyre test team was based.

At Unit 22 as a number two mechanic, Lammenranta began working as front-end outboard – responsible for the upright side of things from the cockpit outwards as the second front-ender would handle the centre of the car. Yet for all that he was a seasoned mechanic at this point, this was another baptism of fire for the Finn.

'Everything about the car is so much more complicated,' he says. 'The F3000 car at that time was manual, not much electronics, and it was a sequential gearbox, so no hydraulics. So it was the complexity of the F1 car itself which was already a massive learning curve to get my head around.

'I was learning again from scratch. You know a little bit of the mechanical stuff but the rest of the car is completely different. There is so much automated stuff in the car, and that's why the steering wheel is full of knobs, so they can adjust everything from dampers to diff pressures. All that is done manually when you take the thing apart on an F3000 car.'

Yet by now clearly a natural, he picked it up in no time. He was moved to the main test team a year later and in 2005 to the race team, an unusually meteoric rise in F1 terms. He made his race debut as front-ender on the T-car – another luxury long since excised from F1. It was the spare ride that teams used to take to races to stand in should serious damage occur to either of the race cars. The experience was instructive, especially in learning the structure of a race weekend – what the practice of actually going racing in F1 entailed.

Having helped out on Juan Pablo Montoya's car that year, he was moved up to the Colombian's crew a year later as a number two rear-ender in 2006. Moving on to the race crew was an important step for the Finn, to be at the very heart of the team.

'It all became a bit more real – this is the race car, so you don't want to make mistakes,' he says. 'You don't want it to break down because of something you have done. It was a big moment, especially because we had very fast cars and were getting results, and it was a great feeling to have built the car that could win a race.'

It was a feeling he would come to know as the very next season he was shifted to become number two front-ender for the most exciting rookie the sport had seen in decades: Lewis Hamilton. He was learning too about the mechanics' relationship with F1 drivers.

'They come and say hello, they know your name,' he says. 'They go around the car and check everybody is OK. The front-ender and the number one might be a little closer to the drivers because the front-ender always straps him in and puts the seat belt on. I was doing that for Lewis in 2007, liaising directly with him if there was something he wanted to adjust in the cockpit. I got on very well with Lewis, he was great to work with and in 2012 I became his number one mechanic. That was a big thing.'

He also enjoyed his first win as a race-car mechanic with Hamilton when the driver who would go on to become a seven-time champion took his debut F1 victory in Canada in 2007. It was another occasion that proved hard to take in for Lammenranta.

'I was overjoyed; it was difficult to describe,' he says. 'I felt that, hold on, I shouldn't be here in the first place and now we have just won a race and I was part of building the car and on the pit crew, so it was disbelief and pride.'

More was to come as Lammenranta experienced the ultimate high the following year when Hamilton secured his first title, coming through on the final corner of the final lap of the final race to take fifth place from Timo Glock at Interlagos to secure it. Thirteen years after taking a chance on going racing in Germany, he was at the heart of a World Championship-winning team.

'That was the first time for me winning the championship and it was the last corner of the last lap,' he recalls. 'At first we were distraught, because we thought we had thrown it away. Then at the last minute we realized Lewis had got past and it went mad. It just went mental; the whole garage went mental. First you explode because you realize you've won it. The smiles were bigger than everyone's faces and then there were tears of joy. It takes some time for it to sink in, though. I was still thinking about it the whole week, telling myself we had just won the championship.'

Now a number one mechanic, Lammenranta's job had changed again. With only one to each car they are very much responsible for the smooth running of their crew. It is to an extent more administrative, a skill absolutely vital to then becoming a chief mechanic. So as well as hands-on supervision they must know the drawings of the car, to understand the specific build specifications for each race, the order of the build and all the attendant paperwork, not least in keeping track of all the parts that are reaching their mileage limits and ensure a smooth flow of new ones – in those days a process that was handwritten and then typed into a computer by Lammenranta.

He once more proved adept at the tasks and in 2017, when chief mechanic Paul James moved to the team manager position, McLaren offered Lammenranta the job which he was proud to take on. It is a position, however, that requires an altogether different skill set to the very much hands-on roles Lammenranta had previously fulfilled.

The F1 chief mechanic is as much a people manager as mechanic because the smooth running and efficiency of both garages is their responsibility and absolutely key to that is the crews doing the work. They must support the twenty number two and number one mechanics under their supervision and ensure that all the correct information and equipment they need is reaching them exactly as required. They must liaise with the design team and vehicle performance team through the race engineers to understand what changes are happening to the car and the areas they affect. All this information is then central to carrying out the successful build of the car in the right spec, before then going on to manage the operation of the cars over the weekend.

THE CHIEF MECHANIC

They must cope with whatever is thrown up, most importantly when things go wrong, to ensure the crews can adapt to problems all the while in a high-intensity, high-stress atmosphere while they are away from their families and putting in long hours. Motivation and people management, then, is as important to the chief mechanic as technical ability is to the mechanics they look after, indeed to a level that many will find surprising.

'I didn't realize what I was getting into,' says Lammenranta with a laugh. 'Some of it is even more administrative stuff people wouldn't think of in an F1 garage. Health and safety becomes your problem. You make sure people are not driving fork lifts without a licence, make sure everyone has the right personal protective equipment, the hi-vis and safety shoes – that was before PPE meant face masks of course …

'But most importantly you have to make sure they are doing well personally too. Now that we have so many races we need to look at how much the guys can take and that they rest because it is just constant now. So we are looking at a way of making it sustainable for them, so they don't say, "I can't be arsed with this any more." So the car crews' wellbeing is one big factor.'

He employs a pleasingly old-school methodology to ensure the smooth running of both crews who will arrive on Wednesday morning to finish off the garage build and start the car build. 'I am going round the garage to make sure everybody knows what they are doing and they have what they need to do it across both cars, all the equipment and all the tools,' explains Lammenranta. 'I get all my paperwork in place. There is an information wall I choose where we have a timetable for everything. It is literally a wall with paperwork on it, usually near the coffee counter. The info wall is there so people can quickly check the schedule for the weekend. It's also electronic of course, and we have a WhatsApp group so I put it there.'

On Thursday he ensures all is well for the fire-up and for legality checks, then pit-stop practice at the end of the day. Lammenranta makes it all happen and adjusts timings if things do not go according to plan, managing the schedule so all the tasks are done in an organized manner.

Once running starts on Friday, Saturday and Sunday, the natural flow of car management begins, with crews adapting to racing scenarios as required. Perhaps most importantly the chief mechanic must be able to manage with alacrity and focus when unplanned events force action. If a driver crashes in qualifying and an engine change is required, the info wall schedule goes out of the window.

'The first thing I do is to figure out in my own head that the changes can be made in the time available,' he says. 'Trying to work with the number one on the order we should do things, to make sure he has enough helping hands, so he can be in charge of getting the car back in working order. If we know already on a Saturday evening we are changing the engine, we would get half started that night, and disconnect hoses and wires. That gives a quicker start for a Sunday morning strip, when you take the engine out and make sure the new engine is ready to go. You need to plumb it all in and fire it all up. If there is a big crash I will jump in and help to give them a fighting chance to get it rebuilt. There are a lot of jobs. It takes about five hours and it really goes fast. That is stressful.'

Finally, on race day before supervising the strip-down, he

still plays a part in the vital pit-stops. Lammenranta can be spotted during a stop standing next to the front jack mechanic. He is one of six crew with a switch to press to clear the driver to leave his box. He is observing all four corners of the car and has the final button to push that releases the car. With sub-2.5-second pit-stops the norm, it is another task where experience is priceless.

It has been some road to reach this point, to have earned such responsibility, to gain all that knowledge, touch, know-how and skill, not least from where Lammenranta began thirty years ago, but he simply could not be happier with how it panned out when he put the farm behind him.

'This is a job where you are constantly learning because motor racing evolves all the time, so absolutely I still enjoy it or I wouldn't do it,' he says with conviction. 'Bad weekends are still painful of course, but when we have a great result, that is what everyone is always after and what makes it. Like the one-two in Monza in 2021. That's why we do it; that's why we are here.'

CHAPTER 18

THE MARKETING DIRECTOR

VICTORIA JOHNSON
MARKETING OPERATIONS DIRECTOR - MERCEDES-AMG PETRONAS F1 TEAM

'My first job in F1 was as a hostess for the BAR Honda team in their motorhome, serving food, tea and coffee. I was doing a full-time degree then which was quite a challenge. After a long day in the motorhome I would go to the driver rooms which were for Takuma Sato and Jenson Button and I would finish my dissertation in there, get a couple of hours' sleep, use their shower and then go and do breakfast. It gave me something; it made me want more.'

Just how far Victoria Johnson, now a stalwart of the Mercedes team, would go in the sport was inconceivable to that twenty-one-year-old back in 2003 when she succeeded in meeting the twin demands of working in F1 and completing her degree. In 2009 she took a full-time job in marketing with the Brawn GP team and since it was bought by Mercedes and transformed into an all-conquering F1 colossus, she has never left the team she now calls home.

In what is by any standards a striking career, Johnson has worked closely with a host of drivers, including four World Champions in Jenson Button, Michael Schumacher, Nico Rosberg and Lewis Hamilton. Not at all bad for a woman who as a girl had considered F1 an almost impossible dream.

The forty-one-year-old was there at the beginning with Brawn, a shoestring affair born of the ashes of the Honda F1 team, with a marketing department of just four people. Johnson now sits at the apex of one of the most successful marketing and branding operations in F1 at Mercedes, with fifty people under her remit and a score of outsourced partners and collaborators. It has been a true success story since she was captivated by F1 while watching it on TV with her dad.

For the marketing operation to work she has had to forge close relationships with the drivers, engaging a spirit of collaboration rather than the combative one where they only reluctantly engage with the marketing requests of their teams. She has a warm, friendly demeanour but also the steely air of confidence and capability that comes with the knowledge that she is very much in control of her domain. There is a professional poise that it is impossible not to admire and suggests she brooks little dissent once she has set her mind on something.

That she has been so successful in her task and that it is vital and appreciated by every member of the team was illustrated amid a shower of champagne at the US Grand Prix in Austin, Texas.

'In 2016 at the US Grand Prix after Lewis won, our team principal Toto Wolff said to me: "You are going on the podium." I was so nervous, I said: "I can't go on the podium,"' she recalls. 'They insisted and then I was in the green room shaking. I just thought, no, no, I was so nervous. I didn't know what I was going to do. Lewis walked in and he said: "Are you coming on the podium with me?" I was so unsure about it, I just said: "I think so."

'Lewis said: "Right, that's fine, no problem." He'd won, so he waited for Nico Rosberg and Danny Ricciardo to go out, then he held my hand, put his arm round my shoulder and took me out there and put me on the step I was meant to stand on and then he went to his step. That's Lewis, he made it perfect. That's what you get from years and years of working together. Then of course he sprayed me with champagne. What a moment.

'When I was that young hostess, I would think: "Oh wow, it's a racing driver!" when I saw them. Now I work with them every day of the week and we are very fortunate to have had amazing drivers like Lewis whom I have worked with for years.'

The extent that the drivers and indeed the Mercedes team principal Wolff consider Johnson a vital cog in the machine might be regarded as surprising. Yet it absolutely reflects the vital importance of the marketing of a racing brand in modern F1, of the financial return it generates and how it shapes almost every aspect of the outward-facing image of the team and why that matters so much.

'F1 is a brilliant marketing platform,' says Johnson. 'From 2018 to 2019 onwards I would say we became one of the leading F1 teams. Because not only did we have car performance and championships behind us but as a marketing team we had all our brand standards up, the look of the car, the team kit, the livery, how we present ourselves at the track with our trucks, our motorhomes.'

This is a vital part of F1. The sport requires money to fund the racing so every team pursues the greenbacks of sponsors with relentless zeal. Securing it is a vital task amid a market that is packed with rivals all vying for the same backing.

'As a marketing team it's about trying to differentiate us from the competition because gaining sponsorship is tough out there,' says Johnson. 'For one brand you will have McLaren, Ferrari, Red Bull all pitching to them, let alone Manchester City, Manchester United, the Olympics. So we want to make the F1 team a desirable asset. To be something people want to partner with.'

This process has never been more important. To present a professional, cohesive and most of all enticing brand to encourage investment has become a fundamental part of the sport. As is recognized at Mercedes, who have eight consecutive constructors' titles under their belts and where Wolff – who is also a co-owner of the team, alongside the Mercedes-Benz group and the chemical company Ineos – knows that it is vital to the team's performance.

'Toto is fully committed, not only to the technical side of our team but the business side of our team,' Johnson explains. 'Not only does he have impeccable taste but also impeccable attention to detail and standards, which is brilliant for me because that means he will push for the same things I push for. The marketing part of the business is very close to his heart. He is really invested, and he wants to see the designs for everything: the team kit, the livery, right down, for example, to the design of the suite we built for the new Las Vegas Grand Prix in 2023.'

This then is where Johnson shines, in what she describes as bringing everything to life. The partners – sponsors – the team have that bring the income, require assets. Their needs, in return for the financial largesse they deliver, have to be met, not least in looking after those assets that are most in demand, the drivers themselves.

This is a tricky road to navigate. Doing anything beyond competing is low down on any F1 driver's priority list and some positively resent every moment they are forced away from the wheel to meet and greet the people paying the bills. Moreover, there are endless demands to do so, all of which must be managed carefully and at every level, as Johnson explains.

'The marketing to driver relationship is really important,' she says. 'If Mercedes want to do a TV commercial, you bring the drivers in at the storyboard stage. You don't get to day one of the shoot and then just say: "You are doing this …" Because you *will* get a bad outcome.

'With team kit I have had Lewis and George Russell in the design meetings and they do the same with the livery, all so they don't get to the launch and say: "Who chose this?" My experience is to take the drivers on the journey with you. Get them to understand the brands and get them involved.'

Which is a technique that has worked at Mercedes, even if it is not easy and not always entirely without bumps in the road.

It delivers outcomes acceptable to drivers and teams alike, and racing is more fun, so they may not enjoy it as such but the best drivers understand it and take part with good grace and commitment.

'There are difficult conversations,' admits Johnson, with a knowing smile. 'But I am fortunate to say that the drivers we have – Michael Schumacher back in the day and Lewis and George now – have been brought up understanding that sponsorship makes a team successful.

'Marketing days with drivers are there because we need the income to finance making a fantastic team. So when you hear stories of other teams where drivers don't want to do marketing, I don't get it, because our drivers understand its importance. I don't have to explain to Lewis or George the importance of Petronas or Mercedes-Benz. When I say to Lewis and George we are going to Malaysia, for Petronas, they don't make a face and go: "Oh, why?" They know they are title sponsors.'

Amidst all this there is also a complex juggling act going on that is often unperceived with a vast range of interests all demanding their own attention. The car that appears on track and indeed every reflection of it, from team uniform to trucks and the very perception of the team, is subject to intense negotiation and development from Johnson and her marketing team.

'We have moved to a majority black livery in recent years. We did it first in 2020 to highlight our commitment to fighting racism and it was a powerful statement,' she says. 'That may seem simple to do but my role in marketing operations is to keep all our stakeholders happy. For example, from a livery perspective, all our stakeholders will have an idea of what needs to be on the car. Mercedes may want a certain look,

Ineos might want more burgundy in certain areas, Petronas more green, and Toto might want something else. If you try to cram those all together without thinking about how they interact with one another, you would get a dog's dinner. I have to create something that looks right for our brand identity, whilst ensuring everyone is represented correctly and therefore keeps everyone happy.'

It may be considered that the idea of brand identity has nothing to do with racing, but in modern F1, a sport where technical and engineering excellence is driven by financial backing, Johnson is playing a role as essential as any. Which is fulsomely acknowledged within every team.

'We have the commercial team that sell our sponsorship and what I am creating is an experience and a look and feel and a desirability so that is where they and we want to be,' she explains. 'F1 is based on both prize money and sponsorship income. I spend quite a bit of money but it in turn creates the brand that brings in that revenue.'

This is a field that has only become more and more important as the popularity of F1 has gone through the roof in recent years. If F1 is a numbers game, those revenue numbers are only increasing and chasing them makes Johnson's task more vital than ever.

'I think back to the figures, what they were worth in 2010, and it's a completely different playing field now,' she says. 'It is huge now, and it has gone up so much because the value of the sport has increased.'

The team's turnover grew from £355.3 million in 2020 to £383.3 million in 2021. With the cost cap in place in 2023 set at £120.8 million, additional income from sponsorship and marketing means the team now turns a profit and can divert funding into areas not restricted by the cap.

The sport has, then, changed dramatically since Johnson enjoyed her first interest in it. She grew up in Thame, Oxfordshire, with a slender connection to motor racing in the family in that Dad owned a crash repair garage that repaired racing cars, run alongside her mum who was an accountant and did the books.

F1 was a Sunday staple in the family home, where Johnson found the sport gripping but a world away from her life. 'I watched it with my dad, and I just liked it as a sport,' she says. 'I liked the excitement around it. I thought it was fascinating, and I thought "Wouldn't that be amazing to be part of that?" Even then I wanted it but I didn't know how.'

She had not even considered F1 as a possible career when beginning studying a business and marketing degree at Oxford Brookes University, which proved to be entirely uninspiring. 'I was never aiming to become a doctor or a scientist, and school for me was just about getting through it,' she explains. 'Then at university I quit after a year to become a holiday rep in Tenerife. I just didn't know what I wanted to do. I found studying so boring as I am just not academic.'

Looking after tourists in the Canary Islands, however, was not as fulfilling as she had hoped, nor indeed did it really reflect her potential. 'After a year and a half in Tenerife I spoke to my dad and he said: "Do you think it's time for you to come back and get a job?" she says. 'I thought he was right and then he saw an ad in *Autosport* for a hostess in F1. He suggested I do that whilst I study because it would be fun and that was it, I took the job and went back to university.'

The gig at BAR Honda followed, itself not without its complications as apart from the hard work, the university began to notice her absence from lectures, which nearly caused her to be failed on her degree. Fortitude and dedication proved decisive, however, as she continued travelling with F1, made the requisite number of lectures and saw out her final year to graduate.

Post-degree, a hopeful career with what was now the Honda F1 team beckoned as a marketing intern only to be dashed as in 2007 they opted to pursue a new concept that did not involve traditional sponsorship; instead, adopting their 'Earth Dreams' idea.

Honda had decided to run a car devoid of conventional sponsorship, instead using artwork depicting the Earth on what they called their 'Earth car'. The intention was an early effort at promoting environmental issues and to bring what they saw as a relevant and ethical image to F1.

To lose her place was devastating for Johnson but she laughs ruefully as she looks back on the experience. The brand-free future experiment would fail in short order when Honda pulled out of F1 at the end of 2008. 'The Earth Dreams concept did put an end to my role. They didn't want any sponsors on the car so they didn't need a full-time marketing junior. It was a shock but it made me stronger,' she says.

Hooked on racing she looked for another route and went to work with the current McLaren Racing CEO Zak Brown who was then running his very successful JMI marketing company. It was a huge player in NASCAR and IndyCar in the US as well as F1 and working with JMI and Brown sealed the deal in convincing her this was undoubtedly the career she wanted.

'It gave me a love for activating sponsorships,' she says. 'I built a good relationship with Zak, and he made me head of special events. I looked after events like him taking people to Le Mans or IndyCar but also on F1 deals too.

'You would work with the marketing department of the F1 team and the marketing department of the client. You are the middleman that brings it all together. I loved it, to keep the F1 team happy and the client happy and deliver maximum return; it was fascinating.'

Yet to be back at the heart of an F1 team itself remained an ambition for Johnson and in 2009 she had her shot in one of the unlikeliest of the sport's success stories. Nick Fry, the CEO at Honda, called to tell her that with Honda's withdrawal from F1 the team had been reformed under technical director Ross Brawn's leadership as Brawn GP. He had bought the team for £1 when the Japanese marque pulled out and now they had Virgin as a sponsor and needed someone to manage the marketing, so Fry had gone to Johnson.

With a Mercedes engine and the Brawn chassis, its remarkable rear diffuser developed intensively for the previous fifteen months as part of Honda, the team would, against all the odds, go on to win the World Championship that season with Button who, alongside Rubens Barrichello, ensured they also secured the constructors' title.

Recognizing the potential and looking to return to F1 as a works team rather than just an engine manufacturer for the first time since 1955, Brawn was bought by Mercedes in 2010 who then took over their headquarters at Brackley. It was the factory where Johnson had begun her career and where she had returned with Brawn. A homecoming for Johnson that meant a lot and since which she has never left.

'It was amazing to walk back in these gates with Brawn because the last time I had left my dreams had been shattered,' she says, sitting in the Mercedes base which has expanded almost beyond recognition since 2009. 'I always wanted to get back team-side eventually and it was a great year because Brawn was an amazing thing to be a part of. We had no money, so sponsorship was really, really critical. It was shaping something from the beginning. I came in as an account manager but I did it all – hospitality, events and partnership delivery as well.'

At Brawn, without Honda's backing, the team was stripped back to a minimum, but their car was a rocket and there was a sense of being part of something special. 'It was a whirlwind,' recalls Johnson. 'Yet it was also F1 in its simplest form. We had scaled everything back, some team kit, some livery, it was really simple but really nice. I am still in touch with Rubens to this day and I knew Jenson from when I was hostessing. They are great guys and we were very lucky to have them as drivers.

'There was a huge sense of camaraderie, which made it a real pleasure. I wonder if I realized at the time just how special that year was? I do now. I was so lucky to have been one of the relatively small number of people that were involved and I have been here [she gestures expansively to the grand Mercedes campus] ever since.'

Since then, Johnson's hand and eye has been an essential part in steering the Mercedes look and how the team is perceived. She is responsible for the grandest projects – like that bespoke Mercedes grandstand-cum-suite at Las Vegas – right down to the design of the team's baseball hats and everything in between.

'We have graphic designers that design the team kit, somebody that liaises with Tommy Hilfiger and Puma to get things produced,' she explains. 'We also have a lot of art workers in-house, so we would do car livery in-house. But there is also team kit and show cars, the merchandise like the caps you see on the drivers' heads. Then on all of it we must ensure the size and order our logos need to be.'

Being responsible for a racing team as a brand might seem a little dry from the outside, but it is a broader and more entertaining church than might be imagined, where one must negotiate compromise between art, business and flair with the talent at the top of the team.

'Well, Lewis and I talk about fashion all the time – he is a fashionista and has an amazing sense of style,' says Johnson. 'But we have to have conversations. We might want him to wear this and he might want to wear that. But we don't pull out the contract and say, "Right, you have to do this,", that's not how we work. Instead it will be: "Right, Lewis, we need you to support Tommy Hilfiger and Puma," and he does. But he might occasionally want to wear an outfit he feels particularly passionate about into the paddock and we support him in that. It's about working with the drivers so they are not on the outside. This job is very collaborative.'

It has been no little journey for Johnson, ever since she tried to make it in the sport she had grown up loving to watch. Her success is a testament to determination and the skills she went on to demonstrate. If Mercedes have been one of the defining forces in modern F1, then Johnson has been a key part of how the team made it and she has absolutely loved it.

'When I was serving tea and coffee at BAR Honda I never once thought I would be part of the structure of this great team,' she says with a smile and the faintest air of disbelief, even after all this time. 'I wouldn't have even known how to do that. Now, just seeing how much we have grown and achieved, I am so proud of what we have done.'

CHAPTER 19

THE ESPORT DRIVER

LUCAS BLAKELEY
ESPORT DRIVER AND WORLD CHAMPION – MCLAREN FORMULA 1 TEAM

'On the last run in quali I had one shot. I did a great lap and banged it on pole with the only set of tyres I had. It was the most pressure I have felt in my life. The adrenaline rush from that; my head down through my arms were tingling, and I could feel the adrenaline in my fingertips. It was electric. That's how intensely you are in the moment while driving; your heart is thumping. Bang! Bang! Bang! It is really, really intense.'

It would be churlish at best to damn a world champion with the faint praise and often unfairly derisory description of merely being a 'gamer'. Lucas Blakeley describes himself as a driver and it's a moniker he has thoroughly earned in the relatively new but burgeoning field of F1 esports. Now a staple at every team, the top drivers are highly sought-after and increasingly supported in as professional, painstaking and comprehensive a fashion as their real-world counterparts. It is best now surely to consign the baggage that posits esports as merely teens playing games in their bedroom to the dustbin of history. F1 has, as ever, taken it to a whole other level.

Ironically, of course, Blakeley did cut his teeth playing video games in his bedroom and unashamedly loved it, but it was discovering that he might put those skills to use in genuine world-class competition that turned out to be a life-changing moment for the twenty-two-year-old Scot. It launched him on a journey to remarkable, and he admits even now, almost unbelievable success.

Driving for the McLaren Shadow team (indeed, all F1 esport competitors are referred to as drivers, rather than players or gamers) and competing on the official F1 game produced by developer Codemasters, Blakeley won the championship in 2022. It was a new dimension to the sport that F1 had only begun in 2017 and Blakeley entered for the first time in 2018. He had tried the traditional route into motorsport, karting, only for the money to run out. When a second shot at it beckoned via the PlayStation, he threw himself into it and it is now his full-time career.

Just what the job entails is eye-opening and a far cry from some casual, albeit terrifically entertaining, button-mashing on Mario Kart. Blakeley and his fellow drivers compete on what they refer to as their 'rig'. A complex and highly technically advanced collection of simulator kit, consisting of a race seat, a force feedback steering wheel – designed to mirror the ones used in race cars – a load-cell pedal set that reacts to pressure rather than distance pushed, all hooked up to a monitor and high-end PC. Yet for all the tech there is also a pleasing, human simplicity to how they interact with the gear few will be aware of, as Blakeley reveals: 'We race in our team jerseys. It's a standard top but for the pedals we just race in our socks. Very thin cotton socks …'

Touch, then, is all in esports and unsurprisingly Blakeley addresses his task with the attention to detail of the most conscientious driver.

'For F1 esports we need everything to be as static as possible. If anything is moving you are going to lack precision and consistency,' he explains. 'I have literally felt my rig was fine, nothing technically wrong, but it wasn't quite aligned with how I wanted it to be. So I completely took it apart and rebuilt it from scratch just to get it millimetre perfect. I had everything in pieces on the floor. It took me six hours to do. Rebuilt everything, all the nuts and bolts, made sure every single bolt was tight, because I want minimum flex and maximum precision. It's small details but worth doing. I am an extreme perfectionist – that's what I do in the pursuit of performance.'

An attitude that drivers such as Michael Schumacher and Lewis Hamilton have embraced to devastating effect. Moreover, Blakeley both has the full support of the team backing him and is putting in the hours to make all the tiny details count.

At McLaren, as with many teams now, there is a dedicated esport studio at the team's headquarters, from where the two drivers per team compete in their online championship. This consists of twelve races over four meetings, with three races each, run on virtual versions of F1 tracks to 50 per cent of a real race distance.

The rig they use at McLaren, then, is identical to the one he uses at home and indeed the one used while competing from home during the coronavirus pandemic of 2020 and 2021. However, now they are back in-house at the McLaren Technology Centre (MTC) in Woking, the team's efforts reflect the seriousness with which the competition is taken.

In the studio the two teammates' rigs are separated by a curtain so they do not distract one another, and behind them sit a line of desks across the room, all equipped with monitors running more high-end PCs under the watchful eye of team members. Here then sits the race engineer, directly behind the drivers, watching the on-board data from the car, the lap splits and all the timings. The task may be virtual but they play the same role as their counterparts.

'They have the same function as F1 race engineers,' says Blakeley. 'They are looking at what the other cars are doing, the pit delta, the undercut, the overcut, the data that I can't see while I am driving. They advise on pitting and we can discuss that during the race just like F1.'

Alongside the engineers is the head strategist, watching the racetrack, checking stop gaps, the rate of change of pace, all useful especially in changeable conditions and will call strategic decisions accordingly by speaking to the race engineers who talk to the drivers via radio. These are vital roles similar to their real-world counterparts but even with some further specialization and are not taken lightly.

'Our head strategist actually works at McLaren F1 – that's his normal job,' says Blakeley. 'He then comes to sim racing as another side of that. He has real-world experience in F1 but also has a background in sim racing, so he is one of the best people for the job. Our race engineers also have backgrounds in the F1 game like ourselves so they know how it works. Every platform in sim racing is unique; you need to know the production, the platform, to know exactly what to look for. Everyone has the right level of background in the right areas, making for a great working unit.'

In F1 esports the drivers represent teams, but the virtual cars they drive are identical in performance, and any differential across the field is entirely down to the driver and his crew, which makes the margins between them disarmingly slight. The gap between P1 and P2 in F1 qualifying is often the gap between P1 and P10 in the virtual world.

'You need the final extra per cent for perfection,' says Blakeley. 'That's what makes the difference. It sounds too marginal but literally a few metres in the race can make the difference.'

He and McLaren, then, are engaged in a relentless pursuit of that edge and it is an unforgiving quest. Blakeley clearly loves what he does but is also committed to extracting the maximum and that means putting in the hours. Two weeks before an esport event he will attend a boot camp at the MTC. The days are long. Arriving at 9 a.m., driving until 1 p.m., with lunch followed by hitting the rig again from two till six, before a break for dinner and getting back to it until around 11 p.m.

'It's intensive but it has to be,' Blakeley admits. 'Sim racing is based on pure driving time; the number of hours people are sitting in rigs driving is crazy. It's pure driving, rinse and repeat, a lot of time and hours. Mentally it is insane. If you are in peak F1 esport season you can be on for anywhere between eight and twelve hours a day. Just in the seat. Doing laps, testing or strategy stuff. There is no restriction on testing like there is in real-life racing. I could do more testing in one day than you might get in weeks in real life. We can do unlimited laps, so that's why the levels are so high and the competition so close.'

There is a commitment here that is echoed throughout F1, from drivers through to every team member. No one goes into this sport half-hearted or indeed half-arsed. Blakeley is no exception in that sense then, but he has also embraced this role with the zeal of a man who feels he has been given a second chance.

He was born and grew up in Irvine, on the coast of the Firth of Clyde in North Ayrshire and still lives there today. He grew up transfixed by cars and then, almost inevitably, F1. When Lewis Hamilton joined the grid in 2007 he had found his hero and an obsession with the sport.

'I remember Lewis in the McLaren; when he came on the scene that was the guy I wanted to support,' he says. 'I still support him to this day. That was my inspiration; I wanted to be the next Lewis Hamilton. Lewis and McLaren were the team I always looked towards. To be a part of that team now, well I have to pinch myself. It's something very special.'

He tried karting when he was seven in 2009 and on his first go out in the wet on slick tyres proved to have quite the touch. Backed by the support of Mum and Dad he competed through the junior categories, but six years later in 2015 they could no longer foot the bill and his hopes of emulating Hamilton ended abruptly and with a crushing and very emotional finality.

'Mum and Dad gave it everything but it didn't work out and it was painful for them to stop,' Blakeley recalls. 'That was really tough, and over the next two years I felt like I had lost my purpose. Racing was what I was; it made me who I was. I felt empty in those years. It's quite a devastating thing because I was so passionate about it, but my obsession and dream was gone and you lose yourself a bit; it took a bit of life out of me.'

This was a low point but much as he did not know it at the time, Blakeley did have another weapon in his armoury, albeit one at that point he had never expected to turn out to be so pivotal. At around the same time he had taken up karting, at home he had also taken to gaming, which he embraced with similar enthusiasm.

'I have always been a gamer, right from my mum and dad's PlayStation One, played games my whole life, played racing games my whole life,' he says. 'I've played every F1 game since 2009 and been using a steering wheel since 2010. I've still got that original wheel.'

While karting at the time was his principal focus, it is instructive to note the commitment he also showed to his virtual endeavours as a kid. 'We made a makeshift wooden platform that I would put the wheel on and I would sit at it in a desk chair with the TV in front of me. It felt amazing, so good, although obviously now the standards are a little higher, but the stand is still in the attic,' he concludes with a smile.

All of which was still not quite realistic enough, however, and he had to go a step further, remembering his childhood fervour with pride. 'Well I was a super-passionate kid about racing and wanting to be an F1 driver,' he says. 'I used to put all my karting kit and my helmet on just to drive round Monaco in my bedroom on the F1 game. I was obsessed with it – all that excitement you have as a kid channelled into one area.'

Which turned out to be time well spent when the karting came to an end. Blakeley was all set for exams and a likely prosaic path to university when he caught the inaugural F1 esport championship in 2017. He describes it as the moment the penny dropped. 'I had always thought I was pretty good at F1 games and at that point it hit me. I thought, "They are there competing because they played the F1 game I have at home as well." It was like pieces of a puzzle coming together.'

A year later working around school and exams, he set about qualifying for the series' Pro Draft – the event where the best are showcased to F1 teams and from which they can select drivers – by setting the quickest time at, as luck would have it, Monaco. Competing with tens of thousands of gamers across the world, he made the time and qualified for the race where the top three would make the draft. On the streets of Monte Carlo again he took third and the fortieth and final place of the year.

'I remember afterwards jumping up and down in my room, losing my mind,' he says. 'I had got into the top forty in the world and I am going to the Pro Draft. I was buzzing, I couldn't believe it. My mum and dad came bursting into the room and were ecstatic.'

A moment of ecstasy that proved sadly short-lived. At the Pro Draft competition at Silverstone he performed well enough but was an unknown quantity with little or no experience. He was not picked – another all too familiar crushing blow.

'I wanted it so badly that I thought I would explode,' he says. 'I went back to the hotel room and cried my eyes out. That was how badly I wanted it, so I levelled it up. I thought, "I will never ever let myself feel how I felt on that day ever again, that rejection, where I felt so lost. I am not going to let it happen." I was hell-bent on it; I have to do this.'

The following year at seventeen years old, fuelled by this combination of determination and hurt, he did little but attend school and drive, every day. He once more made the Pro Draft and in his one race showcase made it count, taking the lead on the outside at Stowe, once more on slicks in the rain, and from there the win. Enough to make his mark this time he was picked for the Racing Point (now Aston Martin) team. A vindication he felt was deserved.

'I put my head in my hands and then I got up out of my seat, and screamed "Yes!" out loud,' he says. 'That was only 10 per cent of the emotion I was feeling. I could have jumped and hit the ceiling, and I was in tears again afterwards. It meant so much just getting the seat. It made me feel that the efforts in karting had not been in vain, and now I was at the start of what I wanted to be a big journey.'

Three years with the team followed. Blakeley was brought in to drive in only a handful of races in 2019 but did claim his first podium. However, he then endured a tough time in 2020, competing from home because of the pandemic, and it was a season he felt he was not delivering on his potential and struggled mentally. Yet it remained a valuable learning experience from which he returned stronger, taking his first win the following year and remaining in the title fight to the death, ultimately claiming third place.

McLaren took notice and signed him for 2022, a moment when he felt his journey had come full circle. 'It was so good to be a McLaren driver. It was a crazy moment, realizing it, given I had grown up watching and supporting the team and Lewis,' he says. 'Imagine telling your eight-year-old self, watching his heroes on TV, that he would be part of that. It was a whirlwind moment and the first time I really felt part of something, part of a family much bigger than myself.'

The task ahead, it became clear, was taken as seriously by his team as it was by Blakeley. He lost 16 kgs between 2021 and 2022 in an attempt to become fitter and leaner to lower his heart rate while competing; to add longevity of concentration without fatigue. Physical aptitude is vital, he insists. 'You get very sweaty during these races,' he says. 'It's physically intense, and people would be amazed if they drove in my rig, because after fifty minutes you are tired. I did eleven-and-a-half hours of driving within twenty-four hours once. It is physical destruction. So yes, to anyone who doesn't think so, it *is* physically demanding.'

On race day he will take a morning run and a cold shower, all aimed at being as calm, relaxed and mentally clear as possible when the lights go out.

The attention to detail preceding a race makes for a familiar methodology in F1. There is practice pre-qualifying then once the grid is set, a consultation with the engineers, before the fine-honing really begins. 'We have a test race with development and test drivers,' he says. 'With six of us practising different strategies, different overtaking, different race starts, I might be in P2 so we would practise driving up for the place off the start, basically doing quick race sims before the real thing.

'We also formulate the final plans depending on strategy and can alter the set-up of the car according to those plans: downforce, ride height, tyre pressures, suspension. Although the cars are identical we would tweak all that for peak performance. It's mainly the wings because everyone is so close on pace. You get a lot of DRS trains because it's very hard to overtake, so you have to be creative with the strategy and how you will overtake.'

As with real life, after the flag has dropped, a full race debrief will then take place to analyse strengths and weaknesses, to learn, to improve.

That he was comfortable at McLaren was clear when Blakeley made a tilt for the title in 2022, an experience he believes sums up why his driving, his sport, is so much more than just a game.

'At the penultimate race of the championship at Interlagos my lead was only five points,' he recalls. 'I had only one set of brand new tyres to try and fight for pole. I needed to pull out one of the best performances of my life. On the last run in quali I had one shot. I did a great lap and banged it on pole with the only set of tyres I had. It was the most pressure I have felt in my life. The adrenaline rush from that, my head down through my arms which were tingling, and I could feel the adrenaline in my fingertips. It was electric. That's how intensely you are in the moment while driving; your heart is thumping: Bang! Bang! Bang! It is really, really intense.'

He duly clinched it at the final race in Abu Dhabi, a moment Blakeley recalls with some pride if not also an endearing air of disbelief that he had come so far, so fast.

'It felt like a whole lifetime had been leading to that,' he says. 'I spent thirteen years of my life, took all that time to get to that point. To win the championship meant everything, every emotion. It was unbelievable and it took three days for my voice to recover after I celebrated.'

One wonders, however, how the rest of the team take to these F1 arrivistes, these garagistas without a garage and their virtual competition, but at McLaren certainly they are welcomed wholeheartedly by the younger generation of drivers who have grown up with gaming. Indeed McLaren's Lando Norris is a keen gamer and Max Verstappen a hugely enthusiastic sim racer who likes nothing more in his spare time than racing online.

'It is so great being part of McLaren. I get to speak to everybody when I am at the MTC. Lando actually watched one of the races at the third event with us in 2022,' he says. 'I was racing and Lando was right behind the whole time watching. He watched and supported us because he wanted to and it was great to have him there.

'He also messaged me before the last race of the season. He said, "Just do what you did yesterday one more time and you have got it, good lad." That was two minutes before the race started. It was really special because I still feel like a normal guy from Irvine, Scotland, so the fact that these guys are communicating with me, it feels amazing.'

Some feeling for that kid from Irvine, who has been on quite the roller coaster in such a short period and for one so young. A journey including some demoralizing lows he readily admits to with great honesty, but from which he came back with fortitude. A testament to his strength of character, then, but Blakeley would not have missed a moment of it, to be part of something so very human and far beyond the pixels that define his competitive world.

'The element of esports that people don't see from the outside, of having a core team atmosphere, the team dynamic at McLaren, that is what is really fantastic,' he says. 'The working relationship, honesty, constructive criticism, all these areas of being a team are really, really important. We learn about one another, there is a great camaraderie, it is strong and it is tight-knit and you know what, you need that to extract the final per cent out of every area. You need that because the margins in F1 esports are so small.'

ACKNOWLEDGEMENTS

This book would not have been possible without the generous provision of time and effort on behalf of all the personnel involved. They were hugely helpful and accommodating and so I offer genuinely heartfelt thanks to Christian Horner, Toto Wolff, Ruth Buscombe, Lando Norris, James Allison, Paul Monaghan, Tom Stallard, Peter Mabon, Marianne Hinson, Rupert Manwaring, Neil Ambrose, Matt Bishop, Frazer Burchell, Russell Braithwaite, Sarah Lacy-Smith, Jack Partridge, Guillaume Rocquelin, Kari Lammenranta, Victoria Johnson and Lucas Blakeley. They told their stories with great honesty and any errors contained herein are mine.

Alongside them and equally vital in the project were the communication departments at their teams who enabled them to take part and facilitated the time I spent with them. They managed this while still competing in a busy F1 season and took on the extra work it entailed with great selflessness and without exception good humour. Their work may not be well recognized outside the paddock, but they are an absolute pleasure to work with and they too deserve my heartfelt thanks. At Mercedes Adam McDaid, Bradley Lord and Rosa Herrero Venegas; at Red Bull Alice Hedworth and Paul Smith; at McLaren Sophie Almeida, Harry Bull and Charlie

Russell; at Ferrari Silvia Hoffer Frangipane and Caterina Cappelli; at Alfa Romeo Katharina Rees; at Aston Martin Will Hings and at Pirelli Anthony Peacock, Davide Casati and Luca Colajanni.

That Damon Hill, a driver who I had long admired and whose opinion I value greatly, agreed to write the foreword was not only an enormous privilege but was also a source of immense pride. He too has my great gratitude.

All my work in F1 has been facilitated by a superb group of colleagues at the *Guardian* and the *Observer* who work tirelessly to deliver an outstanding newspaper and website and in particular those in the office who show such great care and attention to the copy flying in at them, often relentlessly and on very tight deadlines. They too are unsung heroes.

I must also thank my journalist colleagues in F1 who are part and parcel of making covering the sport so fulfilling and indeed entertaining. They know who they are and the press room would be a poorer place in their absence.

On a very personal level I must also thank David Hills and Nicole Hogan, who were there when I first joined the *Observer* in 1999 and who are now great, great friends. We still meet for friendly decompression between races over cold drinks, when they listen with calm, good-natured patience to my tales of cars going round in circles and indeed updates on how this book was progressing. Their friendship has been a rock.

During the long writing process I took inspiration and pleasure in equal measure from the band Fightmilk. Their album *Contender*, a stone-cold classic, was playing all the time and their live shows have been unmissable. They deserve to be huge, if you have read this far, do go the extra step and check them out. Many thanks Lily, Nick, Healey and Alex for making the world a brighter, better place.

My old colleague and friend Oliver Owen took on the task of reading the manuscript and his input was also enormously helpful. Finally, the process of writing was made a genuine pleasure by my editor Ross Hamilton and everyone at Michael O'Mara Books, including Natasha Le Coultre, Ian Greensill, Steve White and Millen Brown-Ewens.

PICTURE CREDITS

Page 1: Damon Hill – corleve/Alamy Stock Photo
Page 2: Christian Horner – Mark Thompson/Getty Images
Page 2: Toto Wolff – Copyright © Mercedes-Benz Grand Prix Limited 2024
Page 3: Ruth Buscome – Alfa Romeo F1 Team Stake
Page 4: Lando Norris – McLaren Formula 1 Team
Page 5: James Allison – Copyright © Mercedes-Benz Grand Prix Limited 2024
Page 6: Paul Monaghan – Mark Thompson/Getty Images
Page 6: Tom Stallard – McLaren Formula 1 Team
Page 7: Peter Mabon – Steven Tee/LAT Images
Page 8: Rupert Manwaring – Scuderia Ferrari
Page 9: Marianne Hinson – McLaren Formula 1 Team
Page 9: Neil Ambrose – Neil Ambrose
Page 10: Matt Bishop – Aston Martin Aramco Cognizant Formula One Team
Page 10: Frazer Burchell – McLaren Formula 1 Team
Page 11: Russell Braithwaite – Copyright © Mercedes-Benz Grand Prix Limited 2024
Page 12: Sarah Lacey-Smith – McLaren Formula 1 Team
Page 13: Jack Partridge – Aston Martin Aramco Cognizant Formula One Team
Page 14: Guillaume Rocquelin – Clive Mason/Getty Images
Page 15: Kari Lammenranta – McLaren Formula 1 Team
Page 16: Victoria Johnson – Copyright © Mercedes-Benz Grand Prix Limited 2024
Page 16: Lucas Blakeley – McLaren Formula 1 Team

INDEX

A

Abu Dhabi Grand Prix 33, 46, 58, 59, 87, 235, 283
aerodynamics 80, 95, 137–49, 212, 241
Alfa Romeo 49–60, 288
Allison, James 50, 73–84, 203–4
Alonso, Fernando 55, 62, 71, 75, 88, 94, 164, 165, 167, 187, 216, 249
Alstom 159
Ambrose, Neil 151–62
Ambrose, Rachel 160
America's Cup 75
Apex Circuit Design 106
Arden International 27, 29
Arnoux, René 236
Aston Martin 58, 92, 114, 164, 165, 172–4, 181, 219–31, 281, 288
Aramco Cognizant 219–31
Astromega 249

Audi 200
Australian Grand Prix 169, 169–70
Autosport 78, 115, 167, 248, 266
The Avengers 238

B

Bambino 66
BAR Honda 259, 267, 271
Barnard, John 78
Barrichello, Rubens 39, 268, 269
BBC 174
Belgian Grand Prix 40
Benetton 74–5, 77–80, 94
Berger, Gerhard 90–1
Bianchi, Jules 65
Bishop, Matt 163–77
Black Lives Matter (BLM) 204
Blakeley, Lucas 273–85

Blancpain Endurance Series 185
Blash, Herbie 128
Blundell, Mark 238
BMW 200
Boat Race 100, 105
Bonnington, Peter 103
Bottas, Valtteri 58, 123
The Boy Made the Difference (Bishop) 176
Brackle 44
Braithwaite, Russell 193–205
Brands Hatch 91, 115, 184
Brawn GP 41, 201, 260, 268–9
Brawn, Ross 41, 268
Brazilian Grand Prix 19, 56, 58, 88, 124
Bridgestone 119
British American Racing 41, 146, 238–9
British Championship 222
British Grand Prix 91, 145, 162, 167, 200
British GT 184
British Junior Championship 222
British Kart Championships 67
Brooking, Antony 181
Brooking, Frederick G 181
Brown, Zak 69, 267–8
Brundle, Martin 175
Brunel University 106
budget cap 95, 193, 196, 202, 203, 250
Burchell, Frazer 68, 179–91
Buscombe, Ruth 49–60
Button, Jenson 41, 94–5, 100, 108, 116, 129–30, 164, 165, 166, 260, 269

C

Cambridge University 50–4, 76–7, 79, 100, 104, 105
Car 168
Carell, Steve 64
Carlin 68
Carluccio's 127
Carpenter, James 182–3
CART/IndyCar 238–9, 267–8
Caterham 114, 144, 147, 152, 160, 184–5
Chapman, Colin 154
Chisora, Derek 128, 130
Clash 22
Clay Pigeon kart track 66
Codemasters 274
Collier, Mike ('Mikey Muscles') 129–31
computational fluid dynamics (CFD) 141–2
computer-aided design (CAD) 155–7
computer games 274–80, 283–5
computer numerical control (CNC) 152–4, 159
Concorde 79
Constructors' Championship: McLaren 169

Mercedes-AMG 36, 38, 199,
   201–2
Red Bull Racing 25, 96–7
Renault 75
Constructors' Championships,
   Red Bull Racing 22
Cooper, John 154
Copse crash 115–16
Coulthard, David 94–5, 233,
   235, 250
Cranfield University 146
Cremin, Jim 168
Cullen, Angela 130

D

DaimlerChrysler 201
Damned 16
Daytona 24 Hours 129
Dennis, Ron 165, 166
Diagonal Communications
   165
Dijon-Prenois 236
dog racing 168
DPR Motorsport 184
Drag Reduction System (DRS)
   54, 283
Dragons' Den 198
Drivers' Championship:
   Mercedes-AMG 36
   Red Bull Racing 22, 24, 153,
   234
   Renault 75
drugs testing 27

Ducarouge, Gérard 238
Dunlop Aviation 79

E

Earth Dreams 267
East Surrey College 182–4
Ecclestone, Bernie 28, 128, 166
Enge, Tomáš 27
Enstone 75

F

Fédération Internationale de
   l'Automobile (FIA) 16, 30,
   54, 96, 169, 172, 203
Feltham Young Offenders
   Institution 174
Ferguson, Sir Alex 31
Ferrari 24, 41, 50, 54–5, 75, 87,
   97, 125–36, 152, 153, 160,
   169, 170, 172–3, 196, 222,
   240, 262
   Maranello factory 54, 55,
   160
FIA, *see* Fédération
   Internationale de
   l'Automobile
Floyd, George 204
F1 Racing 164, 168, 169
Force India 147, 152, 159, 160,
   221, 224
Ford 43, 115, 116

Formula Ford Festival 115
F4 67, 241, 242
Formula One Management 30
F2 224, 242
France 128
Fry, Nick 268
F3 27, 42, 68, 224
F3000 28, 248–52

G

Gascoyne, Mike 146, 147
Gasly, Pierre 233
gay rights 173, 176
German Grand Prix 19
German Touring Car 44
Glock, Timo 253
Goldman Sachs 128
Goodwood 181
Granada TV 201
Grand Prix Drivers' Association 176
Grands Prix 23, 33, 115, 118
Great Ormond Street Children's Hospital 25
GT Cup 184
GT racing 44, 184, 185, 200

H

Haas 50, 55, 238
Häkkinen, Mika 95, 158

Hamilton Commission report 161
Hamilton, Lewis 31, 38–9, 40, 62, 62–3, 72, 87, 103, 114, 123, 158, 161, 164, 165, 166, 170, 172, 176, 204, 240, 253, 260, 261, 264, 270, 278–9
'Hand in the candle' motivation 107
Hatfield Polytechnic 92
Hawkridge, Alex 222
Haymarket Publishing 168
Head, Patrick 104
Heap, Ken 93
Heidfeld, Nick 27
Hill, Damon 11–12, 158, 175
Hinson, Marianne 137–49
Hintsa 130
Hoff, Dilano van 't 65
homophobia 175–6
Honda 41, 187, 259, 267–9, 271
Horner, Christian 19, 21–34, 45, 95, 152
Hulkenberg, Nico 39
Hubert, Anthoine 65
Hungarian Grand Prix 94, 131
HWA DTM 44

I

Imai, Hiroshi 117, 119
IndyCar 238–9, 267–8
Ineos 45, 262, 265

INDEX

Interlagos 124, 170, 253, 283
Italian Grand Prix 68

J

Jabouille, Jean-Pierre 236
Jaguar 28, 54, 92–3
Japanese Grand Prix 65, 217
JMI 267
Johnson, Victoria 259–71
Jordan, Eddie 28, 145
Jordan team 139, 146–7

K

kart racing 26, 66–7, 135, 223–4, 275, 278–80
Kaur, Rupi 60
King, Billie Jean 52
Knockhill 115
Kovalainen, Heikki 166
Kristensen, Tom 27
Kvyat, Daniil 32, 233

L

Lacy-Smith, Sarah 207–18
Lall, Indy 250
Lambiase, Gianpiero ('GP') 103, 109–10, 124
Lammenranta, Kari 245–57
Larrousse 74, 78

Las Vegas Grand Prix 263, 269
Lauda, Niki 37, 91
Le Mans 24 Hours 92, 129, 268
Lechner, Walter 42
Leclerc, Charles 71, 87, 240
Leicester University 200
Little Britain 175
London Scottish RFC 128
Lotus 91, 93, 114, 128, 146, 147, 238

M

Mabon, Peter 113–24
McLaren 24, 29, 38, 51, 54–5, 61–72, 78, 90–1, 93–4, 97, 99–111, 114, 117, 119, 126, 137–49, 165, 166, 169–72, 175, 179–91, 207–18, 240, 245–57, 273–85
  Shadow 274
  Unit 22 251
McLaren Technology Centre (MTC) 108, 170, 276–7, 284
Magnussen, Kevin 175
Maldonado, Pastor 39
Manchester City FC 262
Manchester United FC 31, 262
Manor 56
Mansell, Nigel 26–7, 91, 158
Manwaring, Rupert 125–36
Mario Kart 275
Marko, Helmut 28, 240
Masi, Michael 46

Massa, Felipe 55
Mateschitz, Dietrich 28
Men in Black 83
Mercedes-AMG 24, 35–47, 40, 50, 73–84, 97, 103, 114, 159, 193–205, 224, 259–71
    Brackley factory 199
    Brixworth facility 37
Mercedes High Performance Powertrains 37
Mexican Grand Prix 106
Michelin 250
Minardi 128, 211–12
Minogue, Kylie 64
Monaco Grand Prix 26, 40, 87, 170, 171, 220, 226, 237, 280
Monaghan, Paul ('Pedals') 85–97
Montoya, Juan Pablo 27, 252
Monza 68, 257
Morrison, Brian 116
MotoGP 66
Motoring News 115
Motorsport Valley 159
Multi-21 team orders incident 25
Murray, Gordon 128

N

NASCAR 267
NATO 174
Newey, Adrian 29, 74
Newman/Haas, *see* Haas 238

non-destructive testing (NDT) 215
Norris, Cisca 66
Norris, Lando 61–72, 181, 188–90, 216, 284
Nuffield Health 128

O

Oatley, Neil 93
Olympic Games 99, 100, 101, 105–8, 110, 262
Opel 247–8
Oracle Red Bull Racing 21–34, 85–97, 151–62, 233–44
Österlind, Lars 172
Oxford Brookes University 266

P

PacWest 238
Partridge, Jack 219–31
'people person' position 126
Pérez, Sergio 25
Petronas 35, 73, 193, 259, 264–5
Peugeot 200, 238
Piastri, Oscar 100
Piranha Club 31
Pirelli 113–24, 224
PlayStation 274, 279
pro-am events 128
Pro Draft 280, 281
Prost, Alain 91, 237, 250

Puma 270
Purnell, Tony 28–9, 54

Q

Question Time 174, 175

R

Racing Point 114, 281
Racing Post 168
Racing Pride 176
Raikkonen, Kimi 71, 122, 250
rallying 44, 238
Ratcliffe, Sir Jim 45
Red Bull Advanced Technologies 29
Red Bull Powertrains 29
Red Bull Racing 21–34, 39, 41, 74, 85–97, 103, 109, 114, 120, 122, 124, 151–62, 153, 167, 196, 233–44, 262, 287
racing record 22–3
Red Bull Technology Campus, Milton Keynes 24, 88, 151, 152, 153, 241, 242, 243
Redpath, Pete 159–60
Renault 27, 30, 67–8, 75, 80, 94, 97, 126, 134, 146, 159, 236, 238, 246–8
Renault Spiders 248
Reuters 167–8
Reynard 238

Ricciardo, Daniel 59, 100, 233, 261
Riley 181
Rocquelin, Guillaume ('Rocky') 233–44
Rosberg, Keke 247
Rosberg, Nico 39, 40, 260, 261
Rossi, Valentino 66
Royal Air Force (RAF) 54, 76
Russell, George 40, 71, 263, 264
Russian Grand Prix 190, 218
Rymer, Terry 116

S

'Saint Seb programme' 173
Sainz, Carlos 100, 126–8, 130, 132, 134–6
Sauber, *see* Alfa Romeo
Saudi Arabian Grand Prix 87
Schumacher, Michael 75, 144, 158, 260, 275
schwerpunkt 69
Scott, Dave 78
Scottish Junior Championship 115
Scuderia Ferrari 54, 55, 75, 125–36, 159
Senna, Ayrton 91, 222, 237
Senna, Bruno 39, 88
Shenington 26
Silverstone 115–16, 118, 128, 130, 136, 144–5, 162, 226, 280

Singaporean Grand Prix 90, 131
Smith, Marcus 224
Smith, Will 83
Spa 24 Hours 68, 185
Spanish Grand Prix 19, 32, 40, 122, 131
Spygate 166, 169
Spyker 159
Stallard, Tom 99–111
Stewart, Sir Jackie 41, 115, 167
Stormzy 64
Stroll, Lance 220, 228
Strummer, Joe 22

T

TOCA 116
Toleman 91, 222, 237
Tommy Hilfiger 270
Toro Rosso 32, 114, 126
Touring Car series 44, 116, 184
Toyota 147
Turkish Grand Prix 25, 169
Turner, Callum 209, 215
TVR 212
Tyrrell 128, 167
Tyrrell, Ken 41, 154

U

Ukraine 46
US Grand Prix 40, 55, 106, 261

V

Vauxhall Junior 116
Verstappen, Max 22, 25, 31, 32–3, 46, 71, 72, 87–8, 90, 103, 110, 114, 120, 123–4, 153, 233, 234–6, 235, 240, 244, 284
Vettel, Sebastian 22, 25–6, 58–9, 62, 71, 88–9, 164, 165, 172-5-6, 233–6, 240, 244
Villeneuve, Gilles 236
Virgin 268
VLN Nürburgring Endurance Series 185

W

W Series 165
Wacky Races 16
Walker, Murray 158
Walter Lechner Racing School 42
Webber, Mark 25–6, 116
Welwyn Garden City 104
West Ham United FC 51
West Surrey Racing 106
Wheldon, Dan 116
Whiting, Charlie 54, 128
Williams 44, 104, 159, 250
Williams, Frank 44, 154
Wolff, Toto 19, 31, 35–47, 201, 261, 262
World Championships 23, 26, 39, 60, 166, 253, 260, 268

World Superbike Championship
116
Wurz, Alex 175–6

Y

Yamaha 66

Z

Zip Kart 26